SpringerBriefs in Education

G000049417

Open and Distance Education

Series editors

Insung Jung, International Christian University, Mitaka, Tokyo, Japan
Colin Latchem, Perth, WA, Australia

More information about this series at http://www.springer.com/series/15238

Allison Littlejohn · Nina Hood

Reconceptualising Learning in the Digital Age

The [Un]democratising Potential of MOOCs

 Springer

Allison Littlejohn
Open University
Milton Keynes
UK

Nina Hood
University of Auckland
Auckland
New Zealand

ISSN 2211-1921   ISSN 2211-193X   (electronic)
SpringerBriefs in Education
ISSN 2509-4335   ISSN 2509-4343   (electronic)
SpringerBriefs in Open and Distance Education
ISBN 978-981-10-8892-6   ISBN 978-981-10-8893-3   (eBook)
https://doi.org/10.1007/978-981-10-8893-3

Library of Congress Control Number: 2018936627

Printed on acid-free paper

This Springer imprint is published by the registered company Springer Nature Singapore Pte Ltd. part of Springer Nature
The registered company address is: 152 Beach Road, #21-01/04 Gateway East, Singapore 189721, Singapore

Contents

Summary and Overview

Summary: Massive open online courses (MOOCs) have been signalled as a disruptive and democratising force in education. This book examines these claims, identifying characteristics that influence their development: MOOCs appear to advantage the elite, rather than act as an equaliser; they tend to reproduce formal education, rather than disrupt it; they are designed for those who can learn, rather than opening access for all; and they are measured by metrics that may not be appropriate for open, distance education. These tensions are analysed and potential ways forward are sketched out.

Overview: Massive open online courses have become popular in recent years. The term MOOC has become synonymous with almost any open, online learning. This book identifies specific tensions that exemplify MOOCs and characterise open, online learning in general:

- MOOCs have the potential to democratise education. However, by highlighting prominent universities and organisations, they reinforce the values and extend the influence of the privileged. Open, online learning could be introduced in ways that emphasise the value, knowledge and cultures of all societies and institutes.
- MOOCs have the potential to disrupt education. Yet, rather than being based on a future-focused view of learning, MOOCs often are modelled on the designs and traditions of conventional education. These norms include an expectation that learners intend to complete a course or that they will complete assignments, yet research illustrates that MOOC learners often have very different intentions. MOOC designs could be future-focused to ensure they disrupt education, rather than replicate conventional forms of learning online.
- An important feature of MOOCs is to open access to learning for everyone. Conversely, they are designed in ways that require learners to regulate their own learning even though there is ample research that indicates not everyone has the capability to learn independently. More emphasis should be placed on governments to make sure all citizens have the ability to regulate their learning.

Until this happens, all forms of open, online learning will benefit those who can learn, rather than serving everyone.

- A vision that underscores open, online learning is that learners can follow their own goals. Yet MOOC designs and analytics often are based on predetermined objectives, rather than learner-defined goals. Learners usually are expected to conform to expected 'norms', such as submitting an assignment or completing a course. MOOCs could be designed in ways that allow learners' autonomy and freedom to learn what they want in ways that suit them.

- An important aspect of the vision of people learning autonomously in MOOCs is the idea of drawing on the support of the massive numbers of other learners in the MOOC. Yet these social features of MOOCs often are missing. MOOCs have to be designed to allow learner interaction with other learners and with tutors.

- Data that are used to measure progress in open, online platforms may provide a reductionist view of learner development. Future analytics platforms and tools for open, online learning should capture data in ways that provide a holistic understanding of the learners' intentions and scaffolds to support them in achieving their goals.

- Open, online courses and credentials sometimes are viewed as products for 'consumer' students. This view might oversimplify the notion of learning as a means to transform human thinking and practice. This transformative role of education and learning has to underpin our future planning and policy around open, online learning.

Chapter 1
The Many Guises of MOOCs

Abstract Massive open online courses (MOOCs) often are viewed as synonymous with innovation and openness. In this chapter, we trace their origins and varied manifestations and the ways they are understood. We interrogate the wide-ranging uses and interpretations of the terms massive, open and course, and how these terms are represented in different types of MOOCs. We then identify contradictions associated with MOOC excitement. Despite the initial agenda of MOOCs to open up access to education, it is seen that they tend to attract people with university education. Rather than offering scaffolds that support people who are not able to act as autonomous learners, MOOCs often are designed to be used by people who are already able to learn. Like traditional education systems, MOOCs usually require learners to conform to expected norms, rather than freeing learners to chart their own pathways. These norms sustain the traditional hierarchy between the expert teacher and novice learner (Ross et al. 2014). A particularly troubling feature of MOOCs is that, as supports are becoming automated and technology-based, this power structure is becoming less visible, since it is embedded within the algorithms and analytics that underpin MOOCs.

1.1 Introducing MOOCs

For many readers, MOOCs—massive, open, online courses—need no introduction. The term is generally associated with innovation, openness and democratisation of learning. The term 'MOOC' was first coined in 2008 when it was used to describe the 'Connectivism and Connective Knowledge (CCK08)' course offered by the University of Manitoba in Canada, which attracted over 2200 participants globally (Mackness et al. 2010). The term had entered common parlance by 2012. Indeed, such was the hype around MOOCs that The New York Times pronounced 2012 as 'The Year of the MOOC'.

The excitement surrounding MOOCs is in their potential to open up access to education and allow millions of people around the world to engage in learning. The original idea was that learners could choose how they want to learn and decide their own learning outcomes. Learning is scaffolded by experts, by fellow MOOC learners,

© The Author(s) 2018   1
A. Littlejohn and N. Hood, *Reconceptualising Learning in the Digital Age*,
SpringerBriefs in Open and Distance Education,
https://doi.org/10.1007/978-981-10-8893-3_1

by digital content and analytics-based systems, blurring the distinction between the teacher and the learner and between the human and technology-based supports.

MOOCs have become an industry in their own right. Organisations have been founded to offer MOOCs to millions of learners worldwide. ClassCentral,[1] a website aggregating data and information on MOOCs, listed 30 MOOC providers in 2017. These providers partner with over 700 universities around the world to offer MOOCs. It is estimated that around 58 million students had signed up for at least one MOOC by the end of 2016, with 23 million registering in an MOOC for the first time that year (Shah 2016). It is important to note here that these colossal numbers do not support any specific understanding about the outcomes of these people who signed up for these MOOCs. There is no discussion as to whether the 23 million refers to discrete individuals or 1 million individuals each signing up for 23 MOOCs. Nor is there evidence around how many of the people who enrolled actually participated or learned in each MOOC. Yet, even around 2008–2012, when the evidence of whether and how participants learn in an MOOC was limited, there was large-scale investment in platform and course development.

Despite the phenomenal growth in MOOC numbers and participants, MOOCs are somewhat inconsistent in how they are defined and changeable in the ways they are realised, as will become clear over the course of this book. Over the past 6 years, their purpose, forms and modes of operation have shifted to the extent that the suitability of the acronym is now questionable.

The intention of this book is to examine claims that MOOCs have a disruptive and democratising influence over higher education. However, the effects of MOOCs on education are not as straightforward as they might seem at first glance. An analysis of the literature points to a number of tensions that characterise MOOCs. First, they appear to advantage the [learning] elite, rather than acting as an equaliser. Second, they tend to reproduce traditional formal education, rather than disrupt these. Third, they often are designed for those who can learn, rather than opening access for those who cannot. Fourth, even when learners have the ability to learn autonomously, they often are expected to conform to course norms, rather than determining their own learning strategies and pathways. Fifth, MOOCs are conceived as social networks that allow learners to learn through dialogue with others. MOOCs also tend to be regulated by algorithms and metrics that are based on conventional education, rather than on future-facing forms of learning and these may not be appropriate for open, distance education. Finally, the view of MOOCs as a product for the consumer learner may overly simplify the complex, transformational processes that underscore learning. Over the next five chapters, we describe these tensions and their impact on education. These tensions also underpin in countless areas of open, online learning, so the analysis in this book is applicable to a much wider context of open, online learning than MOOCs. Many of the issues raised in this book are not restricted to MOOCS and have much wider applicability.

We begin with an overview of the rudimentary precepts that define MOOCs and to examine their historical origins in distance learning initiatives and more recently online learning.

---

[1]ClassCentral https://www.class-central.com/.

1.2 MOOC Dimensions

The words that make up the acronym MOOC highlight the fundamental, or at least initially intended, dimensions of an MOOC; that is, they are online courses that facilitate open access to learning at scale (McAuley et al. 2010). MOOCs, at least theoretically, allow anyone with a device and Internet connection, no matter his or her background, prior experience or current context, to access learning opportunities free of charge. The learning experience of an MOOC is designed to provide learners with the flexibility and freedom to chart their own learning journey and to engage in ways that best enable them to reach their personally determined goals. However, the interpretation and employment of the four dimensions of the acronym are not consistent, resulting in considerable variation in purpose, design, learning opportunities and access among different MOOC providers and individual MOOCs. Indeed, their variable employment is influenced and shaped by the different forces and contexts that are shaping MOOCs and changing paradigms and approaches in education in learning. A theme that will be returned to in this chapter and throughout the book.

MOOCs are diversifying. There is increasing diversity both in the variation of MOOC platforms and in the types of learning opportunities on offer (Anderson 2013). The original MOOCs were developed by educationalists using rudimentary tools and platforms (Milligan et al. 2013). These MOOCs were funded through small-scale projects and often staffed by educators volunteering their time and labour. The leap from informal business arrangements to larger scale commercial enterprises took place around 2011–12 when three US-based platform providers opened up: Udacity (www.udacity.com), formed as a for-profit educational organisation, Coursera (www. coursera.com), a spin-out from Stanford University and edX, funded by Harvard University and Massachusetts Institute of Technology (MIT). The UK Government, keen to be seen at the forefront of online learning innovation, founded FutureLearn (www.futureLearn.com) in December 2012, as a for-profit company wholly owned by The Open University.

Since these early platforms were introduced, a variety of online learning providers have turned their attention to MOOCs as the 'next big thing', offering opportunity for pioneering ventures, including the Europe-based Iversity (*iversity*.org) and Australasian platforms Open2Study and OpenLearning. Non-Western MOOC providers are growing in dominance, with the China-based XuetangX (www.xuetangx.com/ global) now the third largest MOOC provider by registered users.

MOOCs are viewed as a blossoming industry. However, despite the millions of learners participating, it has been challenging to identify robust business models to fund MOOCs, particularly when courses are offered free of charge to learners. An early commercial model was based around partnerships with universities and other organisations providing course materials and funding MOOC platform providers to run each MOOC. However, this is expensive for universities and the return on investment is difficult to calculate. Therefore, after an initial rush to be seen to be producing and running MOOCs, some universities began to scale back their investment, possibly because of the limited evidence of return on investment.

New commercial models have been introduced. An increasing number of MOOCs now have credentials and certification as a way to generate income. MOOC learners learn for free but pay a premium for a course certificate. The US MOOC provider Coursera is a leader in this form of income generation. Coursera introduced a 'Signature Track' in 2013, where learners who completed a course were offered an assessment and the possibility of a course certificate for a fee of $49 (USD). It has been estimated that the introduction of certificates generated $8–$12 million in revenue for Coursera in 2014 (Shah 2014), though these figures are difficult to verify. Coursera[2] has since expanded this model as 'Specialisations', a sequence of four to six MOOCs linked by a project or series of tasks that learners must complete in order to earn a certificate. The fee for the certificate ranges from $300 to $600 (USD), depending on the number and cost of the constituent courses, generating the potential for significant revenue.

US-based MOOC provider, Udacity uses a different model. Udacity offers fee-based Nanodegrees, which in 2017 cost $200 per month over 10 months, with a total cost to each learner of $2000 (USD). Udacity also offers college credit and degree programmes. For example, a Masters in Computer Science is offered online through a partnership with Georgia Tech. In 2017, 4000 students were enrolled in the Masters course. Partnerships with universities offer platform providers opportunity to introduce diverse ways to offer course credit, for example through formal accreditation or micro-credentialing.

These examples illustrate how the economic pressures around who funds MOOCs and how these are funded are pushing MOOC designs from their original position of being open access and free of charge towards for-fee, closed, online courses that mimic distance education courses offered by universities. Coursera, edX, Udacity and FutureLearn all now offer courses that are only available to those who pay, challenging notions that 'openness' means 'no cost' and 'access for all'. The platform providers argue that some courses provide a less expensive and more flexible alternative to participating in campus-based degree courses. For example, from 2017, FutureLearn and Deakin University offer full MOOC-based degree courses at a much lower cost compared with studying full-time at Deakin.

Some MOOC platform providers are expanding their business by focusing on the lucrative professional learning and business-to-business market, which has seen MOOC providers partner with companies to create specific courses for their employees. The professional learning area offers the potential for new business streams. For example, Coursera is experimenting with a revenue-generating recruiting service which uses data analytics to connect students with 'positions that match their skills and interests'. Companies are charged a fee for an 'introduction' to a student and the revenue is shared with the university offering the course. The MOOC platform providers are likely to experiment with these and other analytics-based forms of revenue generation to sustain their business.

---

[2]How does Coursera Make Money. Blogpost available from: https://www.edsurge.com/news/2014-10-15-how-does-coursera-make-money.

The practical reality of business models, and the balancing act between costs and benefits that educational institutions have to perform to ensure MOOC sustainability creates tension with the need to open up education to a larger number of learners who need to learn continually throughout their lives. On the one hand, content and accreditation increasingly are viewed by institutions as products that can be sold to student consumers. Course products can be developed, offered and sold in an accountable way. On the other hand, opening up learning requires MOOC participants to behave as active learners. Making sure everyone is able to learn and measuring whether they can is more difficult than simply selling products. Both these positions are viewed as transformative, yet each requires a distinct plan of action. The simplicity of creating and delivering course materials can be more alluring than the complex process of making sure everyone can learn autonomously. There is a danger in overly simplifying how we comprehend and measure 'learning', particularly if swathes of the population are unable to take advantage of the new opportunities for learning that MOOCs offer. However, education sectors have in the past focused effort on advancing those who are already advantaged and MOOCs are rooted in the heritage of education.

1.3 The Origins of MOOCs

MOOCs frequently are positioned as newcomers to, and potential game-changers in, the education world. However, their origins may be traced back over one hundred years to early distance learning enterprises, and more recently to the open education initiatives which arose in the early 2000s. MOOCs have been positioned as hybrids of previous attempts at online distance education, combining early approaches to online distance learning with the scale and potential of open courseware and OER (Gillani and Eynon 2014).

In many ways, MOOCs represent a fresh incarnation of distance learning, which originated in the nineteenth century as correspondence courses using the postal system, and later utilised radio and television broadcasts, and more recently online learning. The first recorded instance of distance learning comes from Boston in 1728, when Caleb Phillips advertised private correspondence courses in the *Boston Gazette*. Correspondence education then expanded extensively throughout the nineteenth century.

The University of London became the first university to offer distance learning degrees in 1858, with several other universities, including the Universities of Oxford and Cambridge in the United Kingdom and Illinois, Wesleyan University and the University of Chicago, offering various extension services in the second half of the nineteenth century. In 1969, the Open University, UK, became the first institution to deliver only distance learning—a model that soon spread to other countries, including Canada, Spain, Germany and Hong Kong. The Open University also pioneered admission without qualifications and the concept of degrees awarded through modular coursework. Students at the Open University engaged with a range of learning media, including specially produced textbooks, radio and later TV programmes broadcast by the British Broadcasting Corporation (BBC), videotapes and in-time computer-based learning.

The advent of the Internet enabled the development of new mechanisms for the dissemination and transmission of content, as well as new open education opportunities, such as open courseware, and open educational resources (OER). In 2001, MIT launched MIT OpenCourseWare, an initiative to put all its educational materials from its undergraduate and postgraduate courses online, allowing anyone to access and use the materials free of charge. OER similarly respond to notions of expiating access to educational resources and knowledge. OER may be conceptualised as:

> Digitised materials offered freely and openly for educators, students, and self-learners to use and reuse for teaching, learning, and research. OER includes learning content, software tools to develop, use, and distribute content, and implementation resources such as open licences. (OECD 2007, p. 10)

The Cape Town Open Education Declaration (2008, available from http://www. capetowndeclaration.org), a founding document of the OER movement, suggests that open education has the potential to 'empower educators to benefit from the best ideas of their colleagues' and to adopt 'new approaches to assessment, accreditation and collaborative learning'. While OER aim to open up access to information and knowledge, a key criticism is that these resources tend to retain the idea of disseminating and broadcasting information as text or video-based resources, rather than drawing on the affordances of the Internet to support learning through active collaboration and knowledge building. This tendency to view educational resources as information to be broadcast has expanded into MOOCs.

MOOCs have the potential to combine notions of distance learning initiatives with open education opportunities, utilising the affordances of the Internet and digital technologies to provide learning opportunities that are open to all, free of charge and regardless of prior experiences and current context. As such, they represent a continuation and combining of existing trends and practices in education. However, the binary view of an MOOC, first as a set of content resources disseminated via the Internet and, second, as an online space for learners to interact as they create knowledge, makes it difficult to conceptualise what it means to be an MOOC.

1.4   Conceptualising What It Means to Be MOOC

The term MOOC is increasingly employed as a catchall phrase to denote a wide range of online learning opportunities. The combinations of technology, pedagogical frameworks and instructional designs vary considerably between individual MOOCs, making it challenging to conceptualise exactly what is meant by the term. Early MOOCs tended, with varying degrees of success, to reproduce offline models of teaching and learning, focusing on the organisation, presentation and dissemination of course material, while drawing on the Internet to open up these opportunities to a wider audience (Margaryan et al. 2015). This model imitates earlier forms of distance learning, where text-based or video-based course materials were distributed to students using postal services. The idea here is that 'learning' (as a noun) comprises materials that can be 'delivered' to students. Other models position 'learning' as a verb. These models utilise the opportunities presented by the Internet and digital technologies and combine these with new pedagogical approaches and the flexibility of OER to design learning experiences where students actively engage in learning activities. What is clear is that there is no single model for MOOC designs.

There have been numerous attempts to develop typologies of MOOCs (Department for Business, Innovation and Skills 2013), and it increasingly is recognised that any attempt at categorisation must embrace multiplicity, acknowledging the diversity and often nuanced distinctions that can be made between MOOC designs, purposes, pedagogical approaches and learners. There have been calls to abandon the MOOC acronym altogether in favour of new titles, which more accurately capture the particular design and purposes of specific courses (Bayne and Ross 2014). MOOCs have been described using a variety of different terms, including 'DOCCs: Distributed Open Collaborative Course' (Jaschik 2013), 'POOCs: Participatory Open Online Course' (Daniel 2012) and 'BOOCS: Big (or Boutique) Open Online Course' (Hickey 2013; Tattersall 2013). MOOCs are not always open and are sometimes available as 'SPOCs: Small Private Online Course' (Hashmi 2013) which may be closed courses available for specific clients, such as corporate training for companies,

In other words, the term 'MOOC' is used to describe a wide range of different types of online learning. The diversity of structure, purpose and designs of MOOCs makes the term of limited use in indicating the educational and learning experiences that MOOCs offer. As will be explored throughout this book, the specific nature and composition of individual MOOCs are profoundly shaped and ultimately the product of their platform and platform provider, designers and instructors, and the participants, who each bring their own frames of reference and contextual frameworks. Furthermore, many of the ideas raised throughout this book in relation to learning, the roles of learners and those responsible for designing and offering the learning, and the structures governing MOOCs are relevant not just to MOOCs but also to online education more generally.

While the concepts and discussion may broadly be relevant to many forms of online education and learning, given that MOOCs serve as the case study for exploring the concepts in this book, it is necessary to explore in greater detail the complexities and variations in design and purpose in MOOCs. The following section will unpack the ways in which the four dimensions of an MOOC—massive, open, online and course—have been variously interpreted and implemented as well as the various theoretical conceptions of MOOCs and how these shape perceptions of their role, the nature of learning and the agency afforded to the different players within them—learners, teachers or instructors, institutional providers, instructional designers and the platforms themselves.

1.5 Shifting Meanings: What Do Massive, Open, Online and Course Really Mean?

While the four words that make up the acronym MOOC collectively work to enhance a democratising agenda, their meanings have become increasingly varied and in certain cases distorted from their original intentions.

1.6 Massive

Massive typically is used in the context of MOOCs to reference the large number of users who can participate in an MOOC. Early discussions of MOOCs focused on the hundreds of thousands of learners signing up for a single MOOC. In this sense, it is closely connected to notions of 'open' and the potential for anyone to access learning opportunities.

The use of the term massive, and the extent to which it accurately represents the reality of MOOCs, has been challenged on a number of grounds. Perhaps most obviously, critics have challenged notions of massive given estimates that fewer than 10% of learners complete a course (Jordan 2015). This suggests that while MOOCs can accommodate large numbers of learners, they have not yet managed to provide consistently high-quality learning opportunities at this scale. Furthermore, the predominance of well-educated, males studying in MOOCs (Zhenghao et al. 2015) has led to questioning around the ability of MOOCs to provide learning opportunities to diverse participants or to truly open up access to education opportunities.

The large number of learners signing up for MOOCs prompts the questions: What does it mean to provide learning on a mass scale? And which pedagogies are effectively able to scale? (Downes 2013; Grover et al. 2013). Ferguson and Sharples (2014, p. 98) suggest that to date 'learning through mass public media is limited in its effectiveness, and successful large-scale online education is expensive to produce and deliver'. Establishing reliably sound pedagogical and instructional design models for disseminating and facilitating learning opportunities at scale to potentially diverse audiences remain elusive. Downes (2013) suggests that consideration must be given not only to the question of content dissemination but also to support meaningful interactions between learners.

Before the advent of MOOCs, Tyler (1993) warned that content 'delivery' cannot exist in isolation from the activities that students engage within in order to learn. Thus, the value of content is related only to the use and interpretation of content in specific contexts. Selwyn (2016) has expanded on Tyler's thesis to suggest that the mass customisation of learning through large, digital systems has led to the primary concern of how to deliver predetermined content to students, with often little 'regard to individuals' relationships with others, and 'the social and political contexts in which they learn and act' (p. 146). That is, MOOCs inadvertently have led to a dehumanisation of teaching and learning and that their success is reliant on finding a way to incorporate and ensure the human element.

This dehumanisation of the learning experience runs counter to the notion of the learner at the centre and the learner determining what and how best they learn. Research has consistently identified solely online learning to be less effective than either blended or offline equivalents (Bettinger and Loeb 2017; Couch et al. 2014; Figlio et al. 2013; Xu and Jaggers 2014). As Dillenbourg et al. (2013) have argued 'massive scale can sometimes be best achieved by aggregating a massive number of small learning cohorts, again highlighting the importance of small group dynamics and the importance of scale-down'. Similarly, the founder of Khan Academy (khanacademy.org), an online learning platform which provides access to videos and mastery-based, sequential learning activities (arguably not an MOOC but certainly fulfilling the criteria for massive, open and online), Sal Khan, argues that the power of the model he has created is not in the online provision of content but rather in the shift in offline pedagogy that the online content provides. That is, having access to high-quality online content and structured learning activities allows teachers to develop more innovative, active, personalised and community-oriented learning activities in the physical classroom setting.

Despite the instructional design and pedagogical challenges associated with online learning at a massive scale, the massive reach of MOOCs does represent a significant opportunity in education. Social interaction is a critical component of learning, but becomes problematic when massive numbers of learners outstrip the numbers tutors. Learners are unlikely to receive tutor feedback; however, Ferguson and Sharples (2014) suggest that, at their best, MOOCs offer learners access to support from a wide range of other learners and facilitate the development of culturally diverse perspectives. The importance of the social aspects of learning and the ability of MOOCs to facilitate this have led to a social learning movement, which lobbies for MOOCs to be designed around social interactions.

1.7 Open

Open education is not a new phenomenon. It first was associated with open universities worldwide and more recently with the broader open movement in education, which among other dimensions incorporates Open Educational Resources (OER) and Open CourseWare (OCW). These are resources freely available to everyone with Internet access, which is an important proposition for many people worldwide. Only 6.7% of the world's 7.4 billion people hold a college or university degree (Barro and Lee 2010). Therefore, OCW, OER, MOOCs and whatever form they may evolve into are important, particularly in developing countries where participation in higher education is low.

'Open' has multiple meanings in relation to MOOCs. It may refer to access; anyone, no matter his or her background, prior experience or current context may enrol in an MOOC (McAuley et al. 2010). Open can also refer to cost; that is, in theory,

MOOCs are available free of charge. Free education was a principle that underpinned the development of the MOOC concept, though in practice many MOOCs are not free of charge (Fischer et al. 2014). The third meaning of open relates to the open nature of knowledge acquisition in an MOOC, including the employment of open educational resources (OER) or Open CourseWare (OCW) which is available under a Creative Commons licence that allows various levels of use (Caswell et al. 2008). The fourth meaning is around knowledge production and the opportunity for the remixing and reuse of resources developed during an MOOC by the instructors and by the learners themselves to create new knowledge (Milligan et al. 2013).

It has been argued that with the rising cost of higher education, the increasing demand for access to higher education and the growing need for people to engage in learning throughout their lives in order to update their knowledge and skills, open education provides a means for reducing economic, geographic and social barriers to participation. In this context, Wilton and Hilton (2009) position openness as a 'prerequisite to changes institutions of higher education need to make in order to remain relevant to the society in which they exist'.

The original notions of openness in MOOCs, where education is free of charge and courses are open to anyone, are being challenged. MOOCs are not always free of charge. MOOC providers have been experimenting with a variety of business models and pricing plans for MOOCs. These include paying for certification, to sit a proctored exam, to receive course credit or to work towards a degree. Providers have recognised the potential of appealing to the lucrative employment market and the willingness of individuals to pay for learning opportunities that lead to greater employability. For example, as mentioned earlier, while MOOC platform providers continue to make most courses and materials available for free, learners may pay for specific services such as certification or closed MOOC-based degree courses. So MOOCs are not always open to anyone. Coursera has found that when money changes hands, completion rate rises sixfold, from approximately 10 to 60% (Onah et al. 2014). It further is not simply the cost that is potentially restricting access but also the time it takes to engage in learning activities.

The current open access model, which allows anyone to enrol in an MOOC, is also being challenged by research showing that not all learners have the necessary autonomy, dispositions or skills to engage fully in an MOOC (Milligan et al. 2013). While notions of the empowered individual and of learner-centred engagement provide alluring visions of what a utopian education system could be, the reality is more complicated. As will be explored in more detail in Chaps. 2 and 3, many learners do not have the extant capability to navigate the informal, largely self-directed nature of learning in MOOCs and the lack of support and interpersonal connections. Increasingly questions are being asked about the balance between effectiveness and openness in MOOCs, questions that will be returned to in chap. 4.

1.8 Online

The online aspect of MOOCs is gradually being blurred, as MOOCs are being used in conjunction with or to supplement in-person school and university classes (Bates 2014; Bruff et al. 2013; Caulfield et al. 2013; Firmin et al. 2014; Holotescu et al. 2014), expanding their scope to include blended learning contexts. In a review of the evidence surrounding the integration of MOOCs into offline learning contexts, Israel (2015) determined that while the blended approach leads to comparable achievement outcomes to traditional classroom settings, their use tended to be associated with lower levels of learner satisfaction. Downes (2013) suggests that for an online course to qualify as an MOOC no required element of the course should have to take place in a specific physical location.

While the online nature of learning in MOOCs is pivotal to their ability to open up learning to ever greater numbers of learners, there are also payoffs, which are often downplayed or disregarded. Selwyn (2016, p. 30) asks the following questions of digital technology:

> Just why should digital education be any more successful in overcoming educational inequality and disadvantage than previous interventions and reforms? Why should the latest digital education be capable of overcoming entrenched patterns of disparity and disadvantage? What is it that makes people believe that digital education will be different?

Selwyn goes on to suggest that there is a:

> Notable dehumanization of the acts of learning and teaching that might be associated with digital education …. current arrangements of digital education often have little to say with regard to individuals' relationships with others, and the social and political contexts in which they learn and act. There is clearly a need to bring the human element of education into technology. (Selwyn 2016, p. 146)

Too often MOOCs are positioned as an autonomous, decontextualised learning activity with little or no connection to the everyday lives and contexts of the learners. However, as will be explored in Chap. 2, the learners' offline context is pivotal to their engagement in and ultimate experience of any online learning activity.

1.9 Course

Downes (2013) suggests three criteria that must be met for an MOOC to be categorised as a course: (1) it is bounded by a start and end date; (2) it is cohered by a common theme or discourse; and (3) it is a progression of ordered events. While MOOCs typically are bounded, this may manifest in different ways. MOOCs initially started as structured courses, designed to parallel in-person, formal learning, such as university classes, with start and end dates. However, an increasing number of MOOCs are not constrained by specific start or end dates (Shah 2015), facilitating a more flexible, self-paced model, which enables learners to complete a course at their own pace. The length of courses also varies, with some constructed as a series of shorter modules, which may be taken independently or added together to form a longer learning experience.

The structure and degree of conformity in patterns of engagement vary substantially among MOOCs. Conole (2013) suggests that participation can range from completely informal, with learners having the autonomy and flexibility to determine and chart their own learning journey, to engagement in a formal course, which operates in a similar manner to offline formal education. Reich (2013) has questioned whether an MOOC is a textbook (a transmitter of static content) or a course because of the conflicts that exist around confined timing and structured versus self-directed learning, the tension between skills-based or content-based objectives, and whether certification is included (or indeed achieved by learners).

Rather than focusing on issues of structured versus unstructured and informal versus formal learning, Siemens (2012) argues that the real tension in how MOOCs are conceived is between the transmission model and the construction model of knowledge and learning. Siemens suggests that rather than being viewed as a course, MOOCs should be conceptualised as a platform on which individual learners construct and ultimately define their own learning.

These different conceptions of each of the terms, massive, open, online and course, reflect the different ideologies and perspectives that drive the expansion of MOOCs. The next section examines various ways these different perspectives have been considered.

1.10 MOOC Ideologies

Various MOOC ideologies can be seen in action, when looking at different MOOC designs, learning activities and formats. Numerous typologies have been developed in the literature, as an attempt to classify these different perspectives (Fig. 1.1). These typologies represent an attempt to capture and classify the manner and presentation of MOOCs.

MOOCs represent a multiplicity of perspectives and plurality of approaches, which means that their value is not always transparent. Examples of these different types of MOOCs are described below.

The early MOOC developers, particularly those who were not experienced in designing for distance learning, designed MOOCs by replicating classroom-based learning. These MOOCs were typified as 'xMOOCs', differentiating them from the earlier 'cMOOCs', which were based on a 'connectivist' (networked) approach to learning. xMOOCs are characterised by learners following a linear pathway through course materials reminiscent of campus-based teaching. These materials include video-based lectures, texts and online, test, based forums, designed to replicate classroom discussions.

cMOOCs vs xMOOCs
- Connectivist MOOCs, or *cMOOCs,* are based on principles of con-structivist pedagogy. Materials are generated by and through inter-actions and collaborations between MOOC participants. The course is designed to function as a network, which is able to intake and pro-cess new information or resources and adapt to these inputs to pro-duce remixable and repurposable materials and knowledge.

- Instructivist MOOCs, or *xMOOCs* focus on more behaviorist models of learning and pedagogy. Information is primarily transmitted from provider to learners, often through short video lecturers, rather than being co-constructed. Learners participate largely autonomously and independently, with limited opportunities (no requirement) to inter-act.

Lane's (2012) 3 part typology
- *Network* MOOCs align with cMOOCs.
- *Content* MOOCs align with xMOOCs
- *Task* MOOCs are focused on problem-based learning, which draws on real world contexts and emphasises application of learning in prac-tice. Skills are demonstrated to learners in a range of presentation formats, combining both instructivist and constructivist principles.

Clark (2013) – 8 part MOOC taxonomy
- *1 Transfer MOOCs* – existing classroom lectures are transferred to a MOOC
- *2 Made MOOCs* – videos, interactive materials and activities are made exclusively for a MOOC
- *3 Synch MOOCs* – have a fixed start and end date
- *4 Asynch MOOCs* –do not have fixed start and end dates, enabling flexibility in engagement and submission
- *5 Adaptive MOOCs* –provide personalised learning experiences, based on dynamic assessment and data gathering during the course
- *6 Group MOOCs* – focus on collaboration in small groups
- *7 Connectivist MOOCs* – information generated and transformed through interpersonal connections across a network of peers
- *8 Mini MOOCs* – are shorter courses, that are less time intensive and attract fewer learners

Importantly, these 8 types within the Clarke Typology are not mutually exclusive.

Fig. 1.1 Common typologies of MOOCs

The earliest Harvard edX MOOCs were designed as xMOOCs, Transfer MOOCs (Clarke Typology) or Content MOOCs (Lane Typology). These courses intentionally were designed to mimic the Harvard on-campus experience (Vale and Littlejohn

2014). For example, Quantitative Methods in Clinical and Public Health Research (PH207X) was designed in 2012 around a campus-based course to teach learners the basic principles of biostatistics and epidemiology, including outcomes measurement, study design options and survey techniques. The Harvard faculty had little experience of distance learning and decided to transfer sections of the face-to-face course onto the edX platform by filming video lecture sequences interspersed with pictorial or interactive illustrations and online articles.

In reality, the MOOC experience is very different from learning on the Harvard campus. Crucially, the sociocultural experience of learning with other students and with the Harvard Faculty is missing. In an attempt to reduce this deficit in their learning some of the PH207X, students used social media tools, such as meetup.com, to self-organise into face-to-face study groups. A meetup in Bangalore drew over 100 MOOC students.

Informal meetups in geographically distributed locations are sometimes designed into an MOOC. For example, the Coursera MOOC, A Life of Happiness and Fulfillment, offered by the Indian School of Business (www.coursera.org/learn/happiness) had meetups designed and orchestrated by the instructor and supplemented by a Facebook group organised by the students. These meetups were reminiscent of distance learning 'summer schools', where students and faculty learning at a distance have the opportunity to interact. In most cases, MOOC faculty are unable to join these meetings, because of the large number and geographic dispersion of these gatherings.

The view of an MOOC as being equivalent to a campus-based course is problematic for learners in countries, such as India or Malaysia, where governments view MOOCs as a way to scale up the higher education system. These governments need to open up education on a massive scale. While MOOCs can open up access to high-quality education for people who have limited options, there should be recognition that learning in an MOOC is qualitatively different from learning on a campus.

These differences in where and how learners and tutors interact illustrate a distinction between online and face-to-face learning. Online learning does not replicate learning while physically present (Selwyn 2014). It offers a distinct experience with potential advantages of distance, time and forms of interaction, but does not provide the same sociocultural experience as learning face-to-face with others. People are not embedded within a learning community in the same way.

Some MOOCs have been designed around communities of people with a shared interest, rather than based on predefined objectives. For example, #PHONAR (phonar. org) is an open, online photography course where learners interact with experts who help them develop online portfolios of photographic images. Learners have to be proactive, taking responsibility for building and nurturing connections with peers and experts and to source resources to support their learning. The decentralised nature of the Internet provides an ideal environment to support the development of an open and participatory culture of knowledge building through collaboration, participation and engagement. In PHONAR, each student sets out personalised learning goals, and the course topics tend to be emergent and responsive to the immediate needs of the learners, rather than pre-prescribed. This approach is different from most MOOCs, where the curriculum and objectives and course content tend to be predefined by the course provider.

Other examples of online courses based around learning communities include crowdsourcing platforms or virtual laboratories where people gather and upload data to a shared platform (Wiggins and Crowston 2011). An example is iSpot (ispot.org.uk), where nature lovers are encouraged to engage in participatory learning by gathering and sharing data on flora and fauna. Active learning opportunities are generated as enthusiasts upload data and experts offer feedback. iSpot is part of OPAL—Open Air Laboratories—an initiative of Imperial College London and The Open University in the UK which aims to encourage people to explore, study, enjoy and protect their local environment. iSpot is not a course in the conventional sense, but it is massive, open and online. Other citizen science, crowdsourcing environments include Galaxy Zoo (www.galaxyzoo.com), where enthusiasts assist professional scientists in the morphological classification of large numbers of galaxies.

MOOCs have been designed around the free flow of data and knowledge. For example, Introduction to Datascience, an MOOC run by the University of Washington and Coursera, focused on learners learning data science by creating and sharing codes. This type of course design is particularly useful for professional development because professionals can learn through engaging in real work tasks, for example, creating code needed for a work task.

Another MOOC that supported the development and exchange of professional knowledge was the Evidence-Based Midwifery Practice MOOC (www.moocformidwives.com) which was led by Midwifery academics in Australia and Denmark in April and May 2015. Midwives located in different countries were encouraged to exchange ideas about how their practice fitted within their diverse geographic and cultural contexts. Professional learning is a growth area for MOOC development, possibly because professionals are likely to have developed ability to engage actively in learning, requiring less support than less experienced learners.

As MOOC designs evolved, some courses were based around and run synchronously with political events. Examples include The Scottish Independence MOOC, run by the University of Edinburgh and FutureLearn in 2014 and the European Culture and Politics MOOC, run by the University of Groningen and FutureLearn in 2016. These MOOCs encouraged participants to consider the implications of Scottish Independence and the impact of Britain leaving the European Union, respectively.

Future MOOCs are likely to make more use of data analytics, virtual reality, simulation and gaming environments. For example, 3D virtual reality (VR) or gaming environments afford students opportunity to collaborate in simulations. Virtual reality is helpful in subjects where visualisation is important, such as molecular modelling in chemistry or building design in architecture. VR supports learning in professional contexts where experimentation in simulated real-life scenarios supports learning, such as nursing or business.

Although VR and gaming are used in these subject areas, there are few examples of MOOCs that are based on VR, gaming and simulations. This possibly is because of the expertise required as well as time limitations for MOOC developers. However, these technologies are on the horizon for integration into MOOCs. Platform providers are experimenting with integrating gaming environments with the MOOC platforms to allow MOOC learners to experience simulations. One example is the EADVENTURE platform, developed by the Universidad Complutense de Madrid to allow non-technical users, including tutors and learners, to create and modify games that can be integrated into the edX platform (Freire et al. 2014).

This section has illustrated the multiple belief systems that underpin MOOCs. These ideologies lead to different approaches that do not always produce the intended outcomes. This book aims to interrogate these belief systems and investigate some of the unplanned, or unseen, consequences.

1.11 The Ambitions of This Book

In this book, we attempt to set out a broad and balanced view of massive open online courses, with a particular focus on questioning the extent to which MOOCs are a disruptive and democratising force in education. This results in an extended focus on the nature and processes of learning in MOOCs and the roles, actions and ontogenies of learners—both as a collective and as individuals.

Chapter 2 introduces the tension in MOOCs between their ability to exponentially increase the number of learners accessing educational opportunities and their ability to provide equal opportunities and outcomes to all those learners. We argue that the majority of MOOCs are designed to be used by people who are already able to learn, thereby excluding learners who are less prepared to learn independently and without direct tutor support. The corollary of this argument is that without taking action to ensure everyone has the ability to engage with and benefit from this expansion of learning opportunities, we will not democratise learning

Chapters 3 and 4 build on Chap. 2 to explore how the emphasis on the individual as active and autonomous learner sometimes conflicts with the expectation that learners conform to accepted norms. This expectation that learners conform to accepted 'ways of being' in an MOOC isolates those who plan their own pathway. We develop a new typology of learner types, which an individual may move between depending on their motivations. We argue that given the centrality of the learner to charting their own engagement and determining their own outcomes, MOOCs must move beyond their current focus on traditional educational approaches and outcomes. This requires the utilisation of sophistical algorithms and analytics that incorporate a human element to ensure learning is not simply scaffolded by course materials and rudimentary analytics, but that there is always a tutor, expert or peer the student can learn with.

Chapter 5 explores notions of quality in MOOCs. It questions whether the current, predominantly traditional metrics and measures are suited to the nature of learning in MOOCs. We argue that the increased reliance on data analytics is skewing how we view quality in MOOCs and that data around learner engagement and interaction has to be interpreted in new ways that are consistent with the new ways of learning in MOOCs, rather than being based on conventional online learning.

Chapter 6 examines the broader societal dimensions fueling the expansion of MOOCs, exploring a tension between the perspective of an MOOC as a set of products (content and credentials) on sale to students with the notion of an MOOC as a means of exchanging knowledge and transforming the learner.

This chapter illustrated that the term 'MOOC' is being used to describe almost any form of online learning. Consequently, many of the ideas raised throughout this book will be applicable not only to MOOCs but also to online learning in general. The MOOC, therefore, operates as a form of educational case study and a backdrop or context against which to position the research and ideas that are pivotal to understanding the changing educational landscape. We hope this critique can stimulate the thinking and debate around MOOCs and online learning.

Acknowledgements The authors wish to thank Vasudha Chaudhari of The Open University for comments and for proofing this chapter.

References

Anderson, T. (2013). Promise and/or peril: MOOCs and open and distance education. *Commonwealth of learning*.

Barro, R. J., & Lee, J. W. (2010). A new data set of educational attainment in the world. *NBER working paper*, *15902*. Available from: http://www.barrolee.com/papers/Barro_Lee_Human_Capital_Update_2012April.pdf.

Bates, T. (2014, October 19). The strengths and weaknesses of MOOCs: Part I [Web log comment]. Retrieved from http://www.tonybates.ca/2014/10/19/the-strengths-and-weaknesses-ofmoocs-part-i/.

Bayne, S., & Ross, J. (2014). MOOC pedagogy. *Massive open online courses: The MOOC revolution*, pp. 23–45.

Bettinger, E., & Loeb, S. (2017). *Promises and pitfalls of online education*. Washington DC: Brookings Institute.

Bruff, D. O., Fisher, D. H., McEwen, K. E., & Smith, B. E. (2013). Wrapping a MOOC: Student perceptions of an experiment in blended learning. *Journal of Online Learning and Teaching, 9*(2), 187–199.

Caswell, T., Henson, S., Jensen, M., & Wiley, D. (2008). Open content and open educational resources: Enabling universal education. *The International Review of Research in Open and Distributed Learning, 9*(1).

Caulfield, M., Collier, A., & Halawa, S. (2013, October 7). Rethinking online community in MOOCs used for blended learning. *EDUCAUSE Review*. Retrieved from http://www.educause.edu/ero/article/rethinking-online-community-moocs-used-blended-learning.

Clark, D. (2013, April 16). *MOOCs: Taxonomy of 8 types of MOOC*. Retrieved from http://donaldclarkplanb.blogspot.co.nz/2013/04/moocs-taxonomy-of-8-types-of-mooc.html.

Conole, G. (2013). MOOCs as disruptive technologies: Strategies for enhancing the learner experience and quality of MOOCs. *RED—Revista de Educación a Distancia, 39*. Available from: http://www.um.es/ead/red/39/conole.pdf.

Couch, K. A., Alpert W. T., & Harmon, O. R. (2014). *Online, blended and classroom teaching of economics principles: A randomized experiment*. University of Connecticut Working Paper.

Daniel, J. (2012). Making sense of MOOCs: Musings in a maze of myth, paradox and possibility. *Journal of Interactive Media in Education, 2012*(3). http://doi.org/10.5334/2012-18.

Department for Business, Innovation and Skills. (2013). *The maturing of the MOOC*. London: Department for Business, Innovation and Skills.

Dillenbourg, P., Fox, A., Kirchner, C., Mitchell, J., & Wirsing, M. (2013). Massive open online courses: Current state and perspectives. In *Manifesto from Dagstuhl Perspectives Workshop*. https://doi.org/10.4230/dagman.4.1.1.

Downes, S. (2013). *The Quality of Massive Open Online Courses*. Available from: http://mooc.efquel.org/files/2013/05/week2-The-quality-of-massive-open-online-courses-StephenDownes.pdf.

Ferguson, R., & Sharples, M. (2014). Innovative pedagogy at massive scale: Teaching and learning in MOOCs. In C. Rensing, S. de Freitas, T. Ley, & P. J. Munoz-Merino (Eds.), *Open learning and teaching in educational communities: 9th European Conference on Technology Enhanced Learning, EC-TEL 2014, Graz, Austria, September 16–19, 2014, Proceedings* (pp. 178–111). Cham, Switzerland: Springer.

Figlio, D., Rush, M., & Yin, L. (2013). Is it live or is it internet? Experimental estimates of the effects of online instruction on student learning. *Journal of Labor Economics, 31*(4), 763–784.

Firmin, R., Schiorring, E., Whitmer, J., Willett, T., Collins, E. D., & Sujitparapitaya, S. (2014). Case study: Using MOOCs for conventional college coursework. *Distance Education, 35*(2), 178–201. https://doi.org/10.1080/01587919.2014.917707.

Fischer, H., Dreisiebner, S., Franken, O., Ebner, M., Kopp, M., & Köhler, T. (2014). Revenue vs. costs of MOOC platforms. Discussion of business models for xMOOC providers, based on empirical findings and experiences during implementation of the project iMooX. In *7th International Conference of Education, Research and Innovation (ICERI2014), IATED* (pp. 2991–3000).

Freire, M., del Blanco, Á., & Fernández-Manjón, B. (2014, April). Serious games as edX MOOC activities. In *Global Engineering Education Conference (EDUCON), 2014, IEEE* (pp. 867–871). IEEE.

Gillani, N., & Eynon, R. (2014). Communication patterns in massively open online courses. *Internet and Higher Education, 23*, 18–26.

Grover, S., Franz, P., Schneider, E., & Pea, R. (2013, June). The MOOC as distributed intelligence: Dimensions of a framework & evaluation of MOOCs. In *Proceedings CSCL* (Vol. 2, pp. 42–5).

Hashmi, A. (2013). HarvardX set to launch second SPOC. *Harvard Crimson*. Available from: http://harvardx.harvard.edu/links/harvardx-set-launch-second-spoc-harvard-crimson-amna-h-hashmi-September-16-2013.

Hickey, D. (2013). On MOOCs, BOOCs, and DOCCs: Innovation in open courses. Available at: http://remediatingassessment.blogspot.co.nz/2013/09/on-moocs-boocs-and-docc-innovation-in.html.

Holotescu, C., Grosseck, G., Cretu, V., & Naaji, A. (2014). Integrating MOOCs in blended courses. In *Proceedings of the International Scientific Conference of eLearning and Software for Education*, Bucharest (pp. 243–250). https://doi.org/10.12753/2066-026x-14-034.

Israel, M. (2015). Effectiveness of integrating MOOCs in traditional classrooms for undergraduate students. *International Review of Research in Open and Distributed Learning, 16*(5), 102–118.

Jaschik, S. (2013). Feminists challenge Moocs with Docc. *Times Higher Education*. Available from: http://www.timeshighereducation.co.uk/news/feminists-challenge-moocs-with-docc/2006596.article.

Jordan, K. (2015). Massive open online course completion rates revisited: Assessment, length and attrition. *International Review of Research in Open and Distributed Learning, 16*(3), 341–358.

Lane, L. (2012). Three kinds of MOOCs. *Lisa's Online Teaching Blog*. Available from: http://lisahistory.net/wordpress/2012/08/three-kinds-of-moocs/.

Mackness, J., Mak, S. F. J., & Williams, R. (2010). The ideals and reality of participating in a MOOC. In L. Dirckinck-Holmfeld, V. Hodgson, C. Jones, M. de Laat, D. McConnell, & T. Ryberg. (Eds.), *Proceedings of the Seventh International Conference on Networked Learning* (pp. 266–275). Lancaster, UK: University of Lancaster.

Margaryan, A., Bianco, M., & Littlejohn, A. (2015). Instructional quality of massive open online courses (MOOCs). *Computers & Education, 80*, 77–83.

McAuley, A., Stewart, B., Siemens, G., & Cormier, D. (2010). *The MOOC model for digital practice.* Available from: https://tinyurl.com/y8rfxzz9.

Milligan, C., Littlejohn, A., & Margaryan, A. (2013). Patterns of engagement in connectivist MOOCs. *MERLOT, 9*(2), 149–159.

OECD. (2007). *Giving knowledge for free: The emergence of open educational resources.* Retrieved from: http://www.oecd.org/document/41/0,3746,en_2649_35845581_38659497_1_1_1_1,00.html.

Onah, D. F., Sinclair, J., & Boyatt, R. (2014). Dropout rates of massive open online courses: behavioural patterns. In *EDULEARN14 Proceedings* (pp. 5825–5834).

Rambe, P., & Moeti, M. (2017). Disrupting and democratising higher education provision or entrenching academic elitism: Towards a model of MOOCs adoption at African Universities. *Educational Technology Research and Development, 65*(3), 631–651.

Reich, J. (2013). MOOC completion and retention in the context of student intent. *EDUCAUSE Review.* Available from: http://er.educause.edu/articles/2014/12/mooc-completion-and-retention-in-the-context-of-student-intent.

Ross, J., Sinclair, C., Knox, J., & Macleod, H. (2014). Teacher experiences and academic identity: The missing components of MOOC pedagogy. *Journal of Online Learning and Teaching, 10*(1), 57.

Selwyn, N. (2014). *Digital technology and the contemporary university: Degrees of digitization.* Routledge.

Selwyn, N. (2016). *Is technology good for education.* Cambridge, UK: Polity Books.

Shah, D. (2014, October 15). How does Coursera make money. *EdSurge.* Available from: https://www.edsurge.com/news/2014-10-15-how-does-coursera-make-money.

Shah, D. (2015, December 28). MOOCs in 2015: Breaking down the numbers. *EdSurge.* Available from: https://www.edsurge.com/news/2015-12-28-moocs-in-2015-breaking-down-the-numbers.

Shah, D. (2016). Less experimentation, more iteration: a review of MOOC stats and trends in 2015. *Class Central, 18.*

Siemens, G. (2012). MOOCs are really a platform. *ELearnSpace.* Available at: http://www.elearnspace.org/blog/2012/07/25/moocs-are-really-a-platform/.

Tattersall, A. (2013) Gold rush or just fool's gold—A quick look at the literature. *ScHARR MOOC Diaries.* Available from http://scharrmoocdiaries.blogspot.co.uk/2013/07/scharr-mooc-diaries-part-xvii-gold-rush.html.

Tyler, K. (1993). Recent developments in radio education. *The English Journal, 28*(3), 193–199.

Vale, K., & Littlejohn, A. (2014). Massive open online courses. In *Reusing open resources: Learning in open networks for work, life and education* (Vol. 138).

Wiggins, A., & Crowston, K. (2011, January). From conservation to crowdsourcing: A typology of citizen science. In *44th Hawaii International Conference on System Sciences (HICSS), 2011* (pp. 1–10). IEEE.

Wilton, D., & Hilton, J. (2009). Openness, dynamic specialization, and the disaggregated future of higher education. *International Review of Research in Open and Distributed Learning, 10* (5).

Xu, D., & Jaggars, S. S. (2014). Performance gaps between online and face-to-face courses: Differences across types of students and academic subject areas. *The Journal of Higher Education, 85*(5), 633–659.

Zhenghao, C., Alcorn, B., Christensen, G., Eriksson, N., Koller, D., & Emanuel, E. (2015). Who's benefiting from MOOCs, and Why? *Harvard Business Review,* September 2015.

Chapter 2
The [Un]Democratisation of Education and Learning

Abstract MOOCs have engendered excitement around their potential to democratise education. They appear to act as a leveller and offer equal opportunity to millions of learners worldwide. Yet, this alluring promise is not wholly achieved by MOOCs. The courses are designed to be used by people who are already able to learn, thereby excluding learners who are unable to learn without direct tutor support. The solutions to this problem tend to focus on the course, as 'learning design' or 'learning analytics'. We argue that effort needs to be focused on the learner directly, supporting him or her to become an autonomous learner. Supporting millions of people to become autonomous learners is complex and costly. This is a problem where education is shaped principally by economic and neoliberal forces, rather than social factors. However, 'automated' solutions may result in attempts to quantify learners' behaviours to fit an 'ideal'. There is a danger that overly simplified solutions aggravate and intensify inequalities of participation.

2.1 The Hype, De-hype and Re-hype of MOOCs

In the past, MOOCs were positioned by governments, universities and other organisations as potential disruptors to the educational status quo. At their most innovative, MOOCs are challenging traditional educational and learning paradigms, where learning typically is teacher-directed and structured within a formal institute. They break down divisions between those who can access prestigious educational institutions and those who cannot, opening up high-quality content to anyone who has an internet connection and device, and providing continued learning opportunities to ever greater numbers. New technological infrastructure and digital technologies are not

© The Author(s) 2018
A. Littlejohn and N. Hood, *Reconceptualising Learning in the Digital Age*,
SpringerBriefs in Open and Distance Education,
https://doi.org/10.1007/978-981-10-8893-3_2

only providing access but also enabling new approaches to learning and the repositioning—if not in practice then theoretically—of learners, educators and institutions. As Selwyn observes:

> the ever-expanding connectivity of digital technology is recasting social arrangements and relations in a more open, democratic, and ultimately empowering manner. (Selwyn 2012, p. 2)

The early promise of MOOCs democratising education and providing future-focused, relevant, high-quality learning for all through improved access and radically new forms of learning may have subsided in recent years, particularly in the Western world. However, the potential of MOOCs and online learning to revolutionise education still dominates the rhetoric, particularly in the developing world where governments are trying to expand higher education rapidly. India alone has expanded its system to accommodate 8 million more students through opening up 20,000 universities and colleges over the period 2001–2011. Corporations and technology companies also recognise the potential of MOOCs to scale up professional training. Private and public organisations seeking to provide much needed continual professional development to upskill their workforce have generated renewed enthusiasm for MOOCs. This excitement was captured The Economist in January 2017, heralding 'The Return of the MOOC' and championing the role that alternative providers must play in solving the problems of cost and credentialing in education ('Equipping people to stay' 2017).

However, the current reality of learning in MOOCs remains somewhat distant from this alluring promise. There continues to be considerable variation both in the nature of learning that MOOCs offer and the ways in which individuals choose to engage with them. As the authors have previously noted:

> The specific nature and composition of individual MOOCs are profoundly shaped and ultimately the product of their designers and instructors, the platform and platform provider, and the participants, all of whom bring their own frames of reference and contextual frameworks. (Hood and Littlejohn 2016, p. 5)

While MOOCs may be pushing boundaries and challenging existing models and paradigms, they also, in many ways, are reinforcing traditional patterns and behaviours in both learning and learners, as well as in institutional structures, ideas that will be returned to throughout the book.

The focus of this chapter is to provide a research-informed exploration of the potential, promise and pitfalls of MOOCs and investigates online and open learning more generally.

2.2   The Learnification of Education; the Wider Context of MOOCs

> We shouldn't underestimate the ways in which language structures possible ways of thinking, doing and reasoning to the detriment of other ways of thinking, doing and reasoning. (Biesta 2009)

Language plays an important role in shaping how we understand and position ourselves in relation to different opportunities and ideas. Nowhere is this more apparent than in the language being used to discuss education and learning. To understand MOOCs, it is necessary to understand, or at least be aware of, the broader educational contexts in which they are being developed. MOOCs not only are responding to technological advances, particularly the social web which has made possible their massive scale and global reach, but also changing political contexts and economic imperatives that call for the expansion of higher education on an exponential scale by using qualitatively new approaches to learning (Liyanagunawardena et al. 2013; Kennedy 2014).

Higher education has been linked to national economic growth, with the most developed economies having the highest proportion of graduates in their population (Hanushek et al. 2008). This link means that populous countries, such as China and India, need to rapidly expand their university sector to ensure capital growth (*ICEF Monitor* 2012). In parallel, the emergence of work practices that are continuously changing and the need to solve bespoke, ill-structured problems under various levels of uncertainty, results in a growing demand for new and adaptive forms of personalised learning that focus on learners and their specific learning needs (Daniel et al. 2015). Many MOOCs, designed as a collection of texts and videos, do not promote this sort of adaptive and personalised learning (Margaryan et al. 2015). Nevertheless, it is understood that these types of courses can have a formative role in higher education, particularly to expand higher education in less economically developed countries, professional learning and training and lifelong learning (Daniel et al. 2015).

The dominant paradigms and approaches surrounding the world of MOOCs are rooted in the contemporary political discourse around education. It is what Biesta (2009) has referred to as the 'learnification of education', or the 'new language of learning'. This new language is framed by the notion that, with the advent of the knowledge society and the exponential development of digital technologies, a new educational paradigm is required; society requires a shift in mindset to focus on notions of lifelong learning, and learner-centric educational models.

As the Commission of European Communities advocated in 1998:

> Placing learners and learning at the centre of education and training methods and processes is by no means a new idea, but in practice, the established framing of pedagogic practices in most formal contexts has privileged teaching rather than learning. (...) In a high-technology knowledge society, this kind of teaching-learning loses efficacy: learners must become proactive and more autonomous, prepared to renew their knowledge continuously and to respond constructively to changing constellations of problems and contexts. The teacher's role becomes one of accompaniment, facilitation, mentoring, support and guid-

ance in the service of learners' own efforts to access, use and ultimately create knowledge. (Commission of the European Communities 1998, p. 9, quoted in Field 2000, p. 136)

Biesta (2009) argues that a new language of learning currently dominates education:

> The 'new language of learning' is manifest, for example, in the redefinition of teaching as the facilitation of learning and of education as the provision of learning opportunities or learning experiences; it can be seen in the use of the word 'learner' instead of 'student' or 'pupil'; it is manifest in the transformation of adult education into adult learning, and in the replacement of 'permanent education' by 'lifelong learning'. (pp. 37–38)

This shift towards the learnification of education extends across the domains of research, policy and practice (Illeris 2009, 2014). The language of learning denotes a new positioning of the role that learning (as opposed to education) plays within society and the economy, and the presumed or desired changing roles and power relations of key players in the traditional education.

MOOCs are at the heart for this changing power structure, promoting a reconceptualisation of the intersection and interplay among the learner, the instructor, the institutional provider and the outcomes of the combined activity and learning provisions. MOOCs, in many ways, are the ultimate encapsulation of this shift towards learning. The earliest discussions of MOOCs focused on the new roles and responsibilities of learners in a networked learning environment where all participants were responsible for contributing to the discourse and knowledge that was shared (Downes 2012). These courses were highly experimental and were considered groundbreaking in the way they enabled learners, rather than teachers and experts, to determine how learning should take place. Their design was based on a network approach to learning, sometimes described as a 'connectivist' (or cMOOC) approach—see Chap. 1 for a typology of MOOCs.

There is currently little evidence to support connectivism as a theory, but it can be considered as an approach to learning conceptualised as participation in a network (Siemens 2014; Downes 2012). It views people as nodes in a digital network, with the connections between nodes as learning. The learner assembles and constructs knowledge within the network, for example, by creating blogposts, microblogposts or other forms of media. These media are shared with other learners and with experts, who can edit or comment. In this way, the connectivist approach has parallels with theories of constructivism, where learners construct knowledge and are guided by a more expert 'teacher'.

A new wave of MOOCs that emerged in 2011 and 2012 were designed around a different, instructivist approach. In instructivist pedagogical practices, the teacher sources and assembles knowledge in the form of artefacts for the student to use. These instructivist MOOCs have been termed xMOOCS. They aimed to allow anyone, anywhere to have access to the same (or similar) sorts of formal education that students experience on campus in universities. Therefore, they were designed around online versions of lectures, readings and discussions that characterise traditional university learning. In reality, the use of these artefacts online is qualitatively different from an on-campus experience. Also many universities have evolved their teaching from courses where students work through a set of materials predefined by the teacher to approaches to learning where the learner constructs knowledge, for example, or 'peer-based learning' where students learn from one another through creating a product or 'studio based teaching' where students build portfolios of work.

This instructivist approach contrasts with the connectivist perspective described earlier. It could be argued that the connectivist approach is more democratic than traditional approaches to online learning, typified by xMOOCS, since it emphasises the importance of the learner, rather than the teacher, assembling and sharing knowledge. However, as we will explore further in this book, cMOOCs may not allow for democratic participation, since the course design presupposes learners are willing to engage in their own learning in specific ways.

Another problem with the cMOOC approach is that some learners do not have the cognitive, behavioural or affective characteristics necessary to actively determine their own learning pathways. Research has provided evidence that learners do not always have the inclination, digital capability or the degree of confidence and self-efficacy required to actively participate (Littlejohn et al. 2016). Thus, the emphasis on the individual as active agent in their learning journey is privileging those who can learn.

Furthermore, the idea of creating knowledge publically and behaving visibly as an expert may lead towards a western cultural approach (Knox 2016), yet MOOC stakeholders claim MOOCs take a 'global' perspective (Godwin-Jones 2014). Thus, the assurance that everyone has the ability to democratically engage in learning in a MOOC is not evident.

In summary, the rhetoric around both cMOOCs and xMOOCs is centred on their ability to democratise learning by enabling anyone, anywhere to access learning opportunities. Yet, MOOC providers and designers repeatedly have downplayed or ignored the critical need for active agency and self-regulation from the learners, and have assumed all learners were equipped to learn independently. Attempts to resolve this problem have focused around designing solutions into the MOOC, rather than focusing on enabling the learner (Guàrdia et al. 2013).

The MOOC represented a new approach, if not to replace, at least to supplement and compliment the old establishments of education. Their conception and promotion is bound in the understanding of the need for new opportunities and new approaches to learning and accreditation that breaks free from the rigid constraints of traditional educational institutions, especially universities. They were seen as taking power away from universities and placing it into the hands of individuals who were able to actively shape their own learning journeys.

Biesta (2009) suggests that there are four trends playing into this new language of learning: (1) new theories of learning and more particularly [neo]constructivist theories that position active student engagement at the heart of learning; (2) postmodern critiques of the notion that education can and should be controlled by teachers; (3) themes of lifelong learning and the need for everyone to continue to learn throughout their life; and (4) the rise of neoliberalism and the prioritisation of the individual, which positions the student as consumer and shifts education from being a right to being a duty. MOOCs appear to respond to all four of the trends Biesta identifies, although perhaps most strongly with the latter two.

MOOCs were built on the emancipatory properties of the new language of learning, suggesting that individuals have the potential and ability to take hold of their own learning. Biesta (2005) suggests that 'Teaching has, for example, become redefined as supporting or facilitating learning, just as education is now often described as the provision of learning opportunities or learning experiences' (p. 55). In this conception, one favoured by policymakers around the world, the learner has agency to determine and shape their own engagement, with the teacher acting as facilitator and the provider a mediator of the learning experience.

This new conception of what it means to learn, how learning should be structured, and the position and role of the individual learner within this is championed by a growing number of organisations. Dua (2013), a Senior Partner at McKinsey & Company, claims:

> What most people—including university leaders—don't yet realize is that this new way of teaching and learning, together with employers' growing frustration with the skills of graduates, is poised to usher in a new credentialing system that may compete with college degrees within a decade. This emerging delivery regime is more than just a distribution mechanism; done right, it promises students faster, more consistent engagement with high-quality content, as well as measurable results. This innovation therefore has the potential to create enormous opportunities for students, employers, and star teachers even as it upends the cost structure and practices of traditional campuses. Capturing the promise of this new world without losing the best of the old will require fresh ways to square radically expanded access to world-class instruction with incentives to create intellectual property and scholarly communities, plus university leaders savvy enough to shape these evolving business models while they still can. (p. 1)

The Economist ("Equipping people to stay" 2017) similarly presents the new possibilities offered by MOOCs and how these are challenging traditional paradigms and institutions:

> The market is innovating to enable workers to learn and earn in new ways. Providers from General Assembly to Pluralsight are building businesses on the promise of boosting and rebooting careers. Massive open online courses (MOOCs) have veered away from lectures on Plato or black holes in favour of courses that make their students more employable. At Udacity and Coursera self-improvers pay for cheap, short programmes that bestow "microcredentials" and "nanodegrees" in, say, self-driving cars or the Android operating system. By offering degrees online, universities are making it easier for professionals to burnish their skills. A single master's programme from Georgia Tech could expand the annual output of computer-science master's degrees in America by close to 10%. (p. 3)

This quote illustrates Biesta's (2009) fourth trend about the neoliberal influence on direction, governance and design of education, as well as how MOOCs are becoming an agent of this societal shift.

Learning, learners and learning outcomes are being reshaped following economic imperatives. The focus is, therefore, on financial benefit, rather than on social growth. They play on notions of the mismanagement of education, as Selwyn (2016) describes:

.... sense of the mismanagement of education by monolithic institutions that are profoundly undemocratic and archaic. These are lumbering organisations where ownership, control and power are concentrated unfairly in the hands of elites – be they vice chancellors and university professors, or school district superintendents, tenured teachers and their unions. Like many large administrations and bureaucracies, these institutions that are believed to be unresponsive, incompetent, untrustworthy, ungrateful, self-serving and greedy. (p. 11)

For the past decades, education increasingly has been dictated principally by economic rather than social or learning imperatives and outcomes (Olssen and Peters 2005), themes that will be explored in the coming chapters at length.

The economic pressures within education are linked to the expansion of higher education. Put simply, educating more students requires more funding. Arguably, the countries that are finding this most difficult are those where university education has been subsidised significantly by the government but this funding has recently been reduced. For example, the United Kingdom, New Zealand, Australia and also Finland, where Finland which recently introduced fees for non-EU students. Funding regimes have changed, and fees have been introduced or dramatically increased, requiring societal changes if the population does not have a culture of paying for or taking out loans to finance educational opportunities. MOOCs are believed to be a solution; however, without clear business models, the economy driving MOOCs has been ambiguous and unsound.

Both Dua (2013) at McKinsey and *The Economist* ('Equipping people to stay' 2017) warn that while a combination of new models and technological infrastructure is facilitating a dramatic shift in the ways in which learning is financed, offered and engaged with, the current reality remains somewhat distant from the promise. However, these now common conceptions of emancipatory learning opportunities and the learner-centred, learner-directed nature of learning opportunities are influencing how learning is structured and how individual learners or students are described and positioned within the MOOC.

However, while the emancipatory aspects of a MOOC are possible, Biesta (2009) warns that:

The absence of explicit attention for the aims and ends of education is the effect of often implicit reliance on a particular 'common sense' view of what education is for. We have to bear in mind, however that what appears as 'common sense' often serves the interests of some groups (much) better than those of others. (p. 36)

In the case of MOOCs, there is a seductive notion of the idea that they are for everyone, making learning and education readily accessible. But the reality is more nuanced than this.

The extent to which MOOCs have actually achieved their democratising mission remains somewhat contentious. MOOCs hold an uncertain space, appearing simultaneously to challenge traditional approaches and paradigms, while continuing to draw on and replicate existing educational and learning models.

The largest providers of MOOCs are still the elite universities and large multinational corporations. And while the language of MOOCs represents the shift to learnification, MOOCs still largely are utilising traditional educational metrics to measure success. What it means to learn has not shifted dramatically from traditional notions or conceptions. Completion and certification of learners still remain the most frequently used metrics for denoting success and quality in a MOOC. A focus undermines the inherent flexibility in the MOOC, which enables individuals to determine and chart their own journey in a MOOC and to self-determine what it means to be successful.

The hint of diversity and self-constructed learning is subsumed within preordained goals and an overarching agenda established by the MOOC creator. This perhaps is particularly apparent in the shift away from openness in MOOCs towards a user-pays model. MOOCs are being subjected to the same pressures and forms of operating that shape traditional institutions. They become a new form of education, with credentialing—an essential element of educational systems—becoming the driving factor.

2.3 Towards Democracy

This chapter has outlined that the democratisation of education can be conceived in several ways:

First, it can be imagined as the expansion of education, facilitating equal access to learning opportunities for everyone. However, as this chapter argued, this form of democracy requires not simply an expansion in the numbers of learners, but also the assurance that everyone has the ability to actively engage in learning. Equality of access does not necessarily equate to equality of participation. Alternatively, democratic learning could be viewed as a shift from teachers and experts deciding what is to be learned and how learning should take place, to learning goals, outcomes and behaviours being at the will of the learners themselves. This section examines each of these perspectives in turn.

At first glance, the expansion of university courses as MOOCs appears to allow everyone (or at least those with access to the web) equal access to learning opportunities. Chapter 1 illustrated that sometimes MOOCs try to replicate conventional higher education in elite institutions (in other words, access to renowned faculties). However, MOOCs cannot offer the grandeur of the physical space of the privileged and influential universities (Knox 2016). The distinction between face-to-face and 'distance' education can serve to downgrade the status of MOOCs, having the impact of making sure MOOC learners are kept 'in their place', and privileging those who are able to be 'present', rather than emphasising equality (ibid). This phenomenon is particularly significant where the university offering a MOOC has unrivaled campus facilities.

Some MOOC platform providers measure learning by identifying whether the learner follows course pathways as directed by the tutors, and whether he or she completes the course. These assumptions about what behaviours indicate whether a student is learning provide little scope for the individual to decide the forms of engagement that are best suited to his or her motivations and needs. Rather than freeing the learner, these measures appear to tie the learner to a specific, predefined learning pathway.

Research tells us that there are many ways learners participate in MOOCs and that they do not always follow course pathways (Milligan et al. 2013). These different forms of participation, detailed in Chap. 4, are manifest in different forms of engagement, ranging from 'active' engagement to 'invisible' involvement, where the course facilitators are not aware of whether or how a participant is learning. The conventional view of education privileges the active approach, and there is empirical evidence that active participants are frustrated by those who these learners do not perceive as active (ibid). Yet, some participants who appear unseen and invisible to other learners and course facilitators report positive experiences of learning. However, this type of behaviour does not fit well with dialogic pedagogies that emphasise people coming together to share their own unique viewpoints, questioning whether learners have a duty to participate actively in education, not only for their own learning but for the learning of others.

To ensure MOOCs support a more democratic form of learning, there needs to be a reconceptualisation of the ways learning goals, outcomes and expected behaviours in MOOCs can be determined by the learners, rather than by teachers.

Yet, it seems the possibility of this reconceptualization is receding. Learning analytics are being embedded into MOOC platforms to measure 'engagement' as defined by the course facilitators, rather than by the learners themselves. Analytics data are visualised in dashboards that measure learner behaviour, completion and achievement in assessments. If a learner chooses to behave or engage in the MOOC in ways that are not predefined and standardised, the data gathered and analysed may give negative signals about the learner. For example, a learner who is actively engaged outside the MOOC platform, or who drops in and out of a MOOC to engage with only what he or she wants to learn, may not appear 'engaged' or 'active' in an analytics dashboard. Some analytics are based on the assumption that there is a correlation between engagement and behavioural activities, such as browsing and exploring, or completion, for example, MOOCs for Development (MOOCs4Dev) analyse all types of engagement within the course platform to assess learner achievement (see https://issuu.com/delta51/docs/mooc_report_final_30_11). However, these assumptions presuppose that the learner wishes to follow a learning pathway predefined by the course designer. If MOOC learning is to be viewed as democratic, these measures and assumptions have to be reconceptualised.

Correlations associated with learner 'completion' are a measure of carrying out the activities determined by the course design, rather than an indicator of what the learner might have learned. This measure assumes that learners want to complete a course or even pass an assessment. However, these assumptions may not be valid in a MOOC. Learners may have set their own learning goals and learned what they wanted to learn, rather than following the course pathway and goals. There are calls to link learning analytics with learning design to ensure that MOOCs are designed to optimise learner progression and completion (see for example Lockyer et al. 2013). However, the idea of adhering to an optimal, standardised design may not allow for democratic behaviours where the learner, rather than the tutor, decides what is to be learned and how. Though what these systems can offer are recommendations for the learner to consider and act upon. For example, recommender systems can suggest readings, further courses or people to link with in a 'just in time' way depending on what the learner is currently learning and how they are learning.

2.4   Different Challenges, Same Outcome

The use of ICT in teaching and learning is becoming a key component in educational policies of developing countries. Arguably, MOOCs can make an impact in terms of opening access to higher education in developing countries, where access rates are low.

The tensions experienced by MOOC learners in the developed countries, for example, the need to be able to learn pro-actively, also affect learners in developing countries. However, some of the challenges associated with ensuring access to education in developing countries are different from those in the developed world and such as poor infrastructure, limited digital capability, social and cultural inequalities and learning and teaching quality issues. Even where people have access to higher education, the quality of learning and teaching may be poor. For example, the government in India has flagged poor quality teaching in some universities, particularly smaller, private institutions, as a key problem in higher education in the country.

Around 4 billion people around the world do not have Internet access. These people are mainly in developing countries, where good digital infrastructure may be restricted to major urban areas and rural areas may have unreliable or no electricity, let alone Internet. In countries like Nigeria or Sri Lanka where students may commute to access Internet Cafes, claims about enhanced learning through MOOCs may not hold true (Anderson 2013).

Even where Internet is available, it may be slow, restricting the ability to stream MOOC content (Liyanagunawardena et al. 2013, p. 4). Access to good digital technology tools can be limited and cost makes these tools less available. Reduced availability to digital tools can limit digital capability within the population, which makes learning in a MOOC difficult. There are also issues associated with cultural diversity. Some developing countries have diverse ethnic communities speaking different languages. India has twenty-two official languages, Zimbabwe sixteen, which makes it challenging to provide equal opportunity to all groups unless they share a common language. People in ethnic minorities can experience discrimination and unequal access to educational opportunities.

Another problem is that some MOOC platforms, such as the for-profit Coursera, operate under strict copyright rules, limiting their use in developing countries. Thus, open-source platforms, such as that used by edX, have the advantage of giving local educators control over the applications, content and curriculum. To address this issue, some MOOC providers, for example, MOOC providers in India supported by the Commonwealth for Learning, are building their own platforms in order to influence developments.

Despite these challenges, MOOCs are viewed in the developing world as a useful mechanism to scale up higher education. There is a recognition that developing nations may lose be vulnerable to neo-colonial effects associated with studying MOOCs largely based on Western knowledge and cultural and philosophical assumptions. This issue has led some governments to develop policy and platforms to expand higher education using ICT and MOOCs.

In India, for example, the government aims rapidly to expanding the higher education system. India is one of the fastest growing economies, yet, only 18% of the population participated in higher education in 2014, compared with 26% in China and 36% in Brazil and over 50% in many developed countries (British Council 2014). By 2020, the Indian government wants to increase the number of higher education places by 14 million to reach a target of 30% participation. To help achieve this goal, the government has invested in the development of a MOOC platform, SWAYAM (Study Webs of Active Learning for Young Aspiring Minds), and courses. By introducing India-focused policy, platform and courses, they aim to address challenges specific to the country.

Some countries have taken a different approach by partnering with international organisations to provide access to higher education in areas where skill shortages have been identified. The World Bank funded an initiative with the Coursera platform to provide MOOCs for students in Tanzania to enable them to develop IT skills relevant for private sector employment tracks (Boga and McGreal 2014). For students in rural areas, the ability to access these MOOCs via mobile phones is crucial. A number of private organisations have sponsored MOOCs as a way to identify future talent for their workforce. Although there are a number of ethical issues associated with this approach, it can be viewed by people, particularly in developing countries where opportunities are limited, to offer huge opportunities. However, while MOOCs go some way in supporting developing countries in facing different educational challenges compared with developed countries, MOOCs still benefit most those who are able to self-regulate their learning, leaving the most disadvantaged behind.

2.5 New Name, Repeating Model

Exploring the myriad of ways MOOCs are being conceptualised and offered prompts the questioning of claims that MOOCs, as a rule, democratise learning. While they are positioned as outside traditional educational provisions and structures, resulting in the ability to shift conventional ways of conceptualising education and learning leading to a redistribution of power, the reality is somewhat different. MOOCs, on the whole, are very much embedded within the existing power structures and the control of the pre-eminent institutions.

MOOCs appear to be a response by the education sector and advocates of open learning to try to retain key aspects of conventional forms of education. The ways in which MOOCs are designed and evaluated tend towards standardised design and normative forms of participation, rather than focusing on personalization and meeting the needs of the learners. In this way, MOOCs are not as open to student needs and may not be as democratic as claimed ideas that will be explored further in the following chapters.

MOOCs in many ways have focused on the potential and affordances of technology to revolutionise education, or at least to shift the balance of power away from traditional institutions and towards individual learners. However, in doing so, they often pay too little attention to the ways in which technology is utilised, both by designers and by the learners. As Kellner (2004) warns:

> Technology itself does not necessarily improve teaching and learning, and will certainly not of itself overcome acute socioeconomic divisions. Indeed, without proper re-visioning for education and without adequate resources, pedagogy and educational practices, technology could be an obstacle or burden to genuine learning and will probably increase rather than overcome existing divisions of power, cultural capital, and wealth. (p. 12)

There is a great deal of rethinking needed before we can consider MOOCs as a form of democratisation of education.

2.6   Concluding Thoughts

The theme of the [un]democratisation of MOOCs is returned to throughout this book. This chapter has explored the tensions that exist between the potential of MOOCs to offer a new reality and order in education, which is more just, fair and open, aligning with the neoliberal agenda of the learnification of education and individualism. However, as we have started to explore, the realities are more complex, in particular the ability for everyone to participate in, and reap the rewards of this new open education. Chapters 3 and 4 will build on these ideas to explore diversity among learners and the variation in learning in MOOCs.

Acknowledgements The authors wish to thank Vicky Murphy of The Open University for comments and for proofing this chapter.

References

Anderson, T. (2013). Promise and/or peril: MOOCs and open and distance education. *Commonwealth of learning*.

Biesta, G. (2005). Against learning. *Nordic Educational Research, 25*(1), 54–66.

Biesta, G. (2009). Good education in an age of measurement: On the need to reconnect with the question of purpose in education. *Education Assessment Evaluation and Accountability, 21*(1), 33–46.

Boga, S., & McGreal, R. (2014). *Introducing MOOCs to Africa: New economy skills for Africa program*. Available from https://auspace.athabascau.ca/bitstream/handle/2149/3473/MOOCs_in_Africa_2014_Boga-McGreal-2.pdf?sequence=1&isAllowed=y.

British Council. (2014). *Understanding India Report*. Retrieved from: https://www.britishcouncil.org/sites/default/files/understanding_india_report.pdf.

Council Canada. Retrieved from http://www.downes.ca/files/Connective_Knowledge-19May2012.pdf.

Daniel, J., Cano, E. V., & Cervera, M. G. (2015). The future of MOOCs: Adaptive learning or business model? *International Journal of Educational Technology in Higher Education, 12*(1), 64–73.

Downes, S. (2012). *Connectivism and connective knowledge: Essays on meaning and learning networks*. Ottawa, ON: National Research.

Dua, A. (2013). College for All. In *Voices on society: The art and science of delivery*. New York: McKinsey & Company. Retrieved from http://voices.mckinseyonsociety.com/college-for-all/.

Equipping people to stay ahead of technological change. (2017, January 14). *The Economist*. Retrieved from https://www.economist.com/news/leaders/21714341-it-easy-say-people-need-keep-learning-throughout-their-careers-practicalities.

Field, J. (2000). *Lifelong learning and the new educational order*. Stoke on Trent, UK: Trentham Books.

Godwin-Jones, R. (2014). Global reach and local practice: The promise of MOOCS. *Language Learning and Technology, 18*(3), 5–15.

Guàrdia, L., Maina, M., & Sangrà, A. (2013). MOOC design principles: A pedagogical approach from the learner's perspective. *eLearning Papers,* (33), 1–6.

Hanushek, E. A., Jamison, E. A., Jamison, D. T., & Woessmann, L. (2008). Education and economic growth. *Education Next, 8*(2), 62–70.

Hood, N., & Littlejohn, A. (2016). *Quality in MOOCs: Surveying the terrain*. Burnaby, Canada: Commonwealth of Learning.

ICEF. (2012, July 16). China and India to produce 40% of global graduates by 2020. *ICEF Monitor*. Retrieved from http://monitor.icef.com/2012/07/china-and-india-to-produce-40-of-global-graduates-by-2020/.

Illeris, K. (Ed.). (2009). *Contemporary theories of learning: learning theorists… in their own words*. London, UK: Routledge.

Illeris, K. (2014). Transformative learning and identity. *Journal of Transformative Education, 12*(2), 148–163.

Kellner, D. (2004). Technological transformation, multiple literacies, and the re-visioning of education. *E-Learning, 1*(1), 9–37.

Kennedy, J. (2014). Characteristics of massive open online courses (MOOCs): A research review, 2009–2012. *Journal of Interactive Online Learning, 13*(1), 1–15.

Knox, J. (2016). *Posthumanism and the massive open online course: Contaminating the subject of global education*. New York, NY: Routledge.

Littlejohn, A., Hood, N., Milligan, C., & Mustain, P. (2016). Learning in MOOCs: Motivations and self-regulated learning in MOOCs. *The Internet and Higher Education, 29*, 40–48. Retrieved from http://dx.doi.org/10.1016/j.iheduc.2015.12.003.

Liyanagunawardena, T. R., Adams, A. A., & Williams, S. A. (2013). MOOCs: A systematic study of the published literature 2008–2012. *The International Review of Research in Open and Distributed Learning, 14*(3), 202–227.

Lockyer, L., Heathcote, E., & Dawson, S. (2013). Informing pedagogical action: Aligning learning analytics with learning design. *American Behavioral Scientist, 57*(10), 1439–1459.

Margaryan, A., Bianco, M., & Littlejohn, A. (2015). Instructional quality of massive open online courses (MOOCs). *Computers & Education, 80*, 77–83.

Milligan, C., Margaryan, A., & Littlejohn, A. (2013). Patterns of engagement in connectivist MOOCs. *Journal of Online Learning and Teaching, 9* (2), 149–159. Retrieved from http://jolt.merlot.org/vol9no2/milligan_0613.htm.

Olssen, M., & Peters, M. A. (2005). Neoliberalism, higher education and the knowledge economy: From the free market to knowledge capitalism. *Journal of education policy, 20*(3), 313–345.

Selwyn, N. (2012). *Education in a digital world: Global perspectives on technology and education.* New York, NY: Routledge.

Selwyn, N. (2016). *Is technology good for education.* Cambridge, UK: Polity Books.

Siemens, G. (2014). Connectivism: A learning theory for the digital age. *International Journal of Instructional Technology and Distance Learning, 2*(1). Retrieved from http://www.itdl.org/Journal/Jan_05/article01.htm.

Chapter 3
The Emancipated Learner? The Tensions Facing Learners in Massive, Open Learning

Abstract MOOCs have the potential to challenge existing educational models. Paradoxically, they frequently reinforce educational conventions by requiring the learners to conform to expected norms of current educational models. Recent research has produced data on how learners engage in MOOCs. And yet, despite the extensive data, rather than freeing learners to chart their own pathways, MOOCs still require the learners to conform to expected norms. The very act of learning autonomously often causes tensions, most noticeably when learners choose to drop out, rather than complete a course as expected, or when they engage in MOOCs as mere observers, rather than active contributors. In this chapter, we explore how the emphasis on the individual as active and autonomous learner sometimes conflicts with the expectation that learners conform to accepted norms. This expectation that learners conform to accepted 'ways of being' in a MOOC isolates those who plan their own pathway. The chapter concludes with a typology of different learners, arguing that, rather than adhering to a 'type', each MOOC participant moves across these learner types, depending on their motivations, and may span different types, rather than falling into one single category.

3.1 Individual Learner, Common Challenges

MOOCs have the potential to provide as many different learning experiences as there are learners. Each learner engages differently, guided and influenced by their own motivations and goals. Chapter two explored this potential of MOOCs as a move from conventional 'education' to broader forms of 'learnification'. In this chapter, these ideas are extended to explore how changes in language are shaping our understanding and conceptualisation of what it means to engage in a MOOC (or learning more generally) and how this influences the process and product of the

© The Author(s) 2018
A. Littlejohn and N. Hood, *Reconceptualising Learning in the Digital Age*,
SpringerBriefs in Open and Distance Education,
https://doi.org/10.1007/978-981-10-8893-3_3

MOOC experience. Embedded within this new learning are assumptions about what it means to be a learner, and in particular the myth of the universal learner.[1]

Biesta (2009) suggests that the move towards the learnification of education acts to emphasise the centrality of the individual learner, not only in the learning process but also within the structures that shape and mediate learning experiences. This apparent focus on the learner and learner-centred or learner-oriented design is devised to suggest an empowerment of the learner and their emancipation from traditional institutions that controlled education. This chapter will explore how these ideas are shaping the concepts of learners and learning in MOOCs, in particular picking up on Biesta's warning of the dangers in subscribing to this idea.

Rensfeldt (2012) has suggested that technology and networked learning have contributed to this 'radical shift in favour of the individual learner, where personalisation is considered to challenge the dominant view of the enclosed, mass treatment by educational institutions' (p. 407). Selwyn (2016) argues that while this focus on the learner and learner choice is typically equated with giving control back to individuals, the reality is somewhat different. It rather emphasises the role of market values and the positioning of learner as product and the packaging of education for a consumer society with 'its emphasis on self-expression and lifestyle choices through individualistic acts of consumption' (p. 79).

In this chapter, we position the learner within the discourse on MOOCs. We examine the motivations, learning dispositions and behaviours of learners and what the research demonstrates as the best ways to support individual and collective learning journeys. We start by considering distinctive ways the learner is perceived by different stakeholders.

3.2 Student, Learner, User, Participant—Multiple Names for Multiple Actors

A range of terms have been used to denote people taking a MOOC: learner; student; user; participant. Typically, they are employed uncritically and interchangeably. Rarely are the terms or how they shape our understanding of the role, agency and position of the individuals they name interrogated. Biesta (2009) suggests that what we call those who are the subject of education matters. Not because language has a particular power but because the use of a particular word leads more easily to other words, and therefore becomes connected, often unconsciously, to certain meanings and assumptions. Biesta (2009) emphasises the importance of the labels attributed to those who are the receivers of education. What we call those who are the subject of education matters. This is not only because language can be powerful, but also because these labels are open to interpretation and could lead, unconsciously, to mis-

---

[1]Todd Rose, The Myth of the Universal Learner Available from: https://www.vteducation. org/en/articles/collaborating-technology-and-active-learning/myth-universal-learner-todd-rose-variability.

construed meanings and assumptions. For instance—if the MOOC learner is labelled as a 'student', it may conjure images of someone who has signed up to complete a course. The learner may also be considered a 'consumer' who would be willing to pay a fee to participate in a MOOC. These terms, 'student' and 'consumer', signify different values.

Language and the words we use determine what can (and cannot) be done and what is (and what is not) possible. What we choose to label those individuals engaging in a MOOC influences how we position these individuals in relation to each other, to the teacher, to the content and instructional design, to the technology, to the platform provider, to the outcomes that they achieve or attain.

The choice of language around individuals extends to further encapsulate the terms used to describe different components of the learning journey. Successful completion, engagement, interaction, learning, achievement, accreditation are all used to denote the desired behaviour and to shape the methods of participating in the learning space of MOOCs.

Traditionally, the subjects of any educational experience, or those belonging to any educational system are unequivocally referred to as 'students' As students enrolled in a programme of study at an institution (be it offline, online or in a blended setting), there is consensus as to the overarching purpose of their engagement and activity, and in many cases a relatively linear trajectory of their educational experience. The student is positioned as the subject of education, the one who is summoned to study. As a subject of education, they are situated as part of a formal, hierarchical educational system, which has rules, regulations and outcomes that are externally determined.

3.2.1 The Student, the Learner

From the new language of learning perspective, the student is less subject than object, lacking the agency to chart their own educational experiences or to shape their learning journey. They, however, operate from a position within the system and by virtue of being a member of an established institution are offered a degree of legitimacy. The extent to which an individual enrolled in a MOOC might be labelled a student is contested. MOOCs can operate within or outside of established institutions, educational frameworks and traditional structures. And this fluidity in the positioning of MOOCs and the considerable plurality in the agendas, motivations and goals of individuals enrolled in them makes it challenging to position the learning experience of enrollees within traditional educational structures, and often the institution providing the MOOC in which the student is enrolled.

'Learner' is increasingly used in formal and informal, online and offline learning contexts. Part of its popularity is the notion that the learner is an active agent who has control over and takes responsibility for their educational journey and in determining their learning experience. Although the ability (or inability) of all learners participating in MOOCs to become active agents and determiners of their own learning journeys will be explored in Chap. 4. The 'student-led' nature of learning is further emphasised through the (desired) merging of roles between teacher and learner in MOOCs. That is, MOOCs frequently position participants not only in the role of students but also as teachers who are supposed to take responsibility for supporting the learning and development of other participants. For example, in Chapter One we described how 'cMOOCS' are designed such that students learn by contributing and sharing knowledge within the MOOC network. Some MOOCs have peer-review mechanisms, where students are expected to provide constructive feedback on assignments, and projects. Alternately, within MOOC discussion forums, learners voluntarily take up the role of being moderators, or Teaching Assistants. This idea of social learning in a MOOC, where massive numbers of participants act as students and, at the same time, teachers of others, has been underscored in Chap. 1 as one of the most important features of MOOCs (Ferguson and Sharples 2014).

While this model of collaborative, socially constructed and collectively determined learning and the fluid movement between roles is, to many, an appealing notion, its manifestation in reality is more questionable. Studies suggests that majority of learners in MOOCs operate as isolated individuals (Hew and Cheung 2014), firmly identifying with the role of learner, rather than taking responsibility to contribute to the collective learning and knowledge building of all MOOC participants. This may seem surprising because these notions of agency and self-determination frequently are used to represent a liberation of the learner from traditional power structures in education, from the dominance of the institution and a top-down educational approach where the teacher controls and determines the nature of the experience within the tightly controlled guidelines of the accrediting institution. Perhaps the learner does not always want to be emancipated.

In traditional models of education the agenda is controlled by institutions who determine the inputs, processes and outcomes of learning. Selwyn (2016) suggests that connectivity of digital technologies has the potential to recast social arrangements in education. Online learning is positioned in opposition to this apparent 'top-down' traditional model. He claims:

> Such descriptions are intended to convey a sense of the mismanagement of education by monolithic institutions that are profoundly undemocratic and archaic. These are lumbering organisations where ownership, control and power are concentrated unfairly in the hands of elites – be they vice chancellors and university professors, or school district superintendents, tenured teachers and their unions. Like many large administrations and bureacracies, these institutions that are believed to be unresponsive, incompetent, untrustworthy, ungrateful, self-serving and greedy. (Selwyn 2016, p. 11)

The narrative of the broken system, and the transition of power and agency from institutions to individuals belie the common reality of a perpetration of existing models in MOOCs. Selwyn (2014) warns that the reality is a continuation of the existing hierarchy, from those that 'do' educational technology (traditional institutions and the new-comers technology companies) to those who have educational technology 'done to them'.

The term 'learner' has particular appeal in the context of MOOCs because of the supposed potential of MOOCs to disrupt traditional tenets and structures of education. Open and flexible enrolments result in diverse demographics which, in turn, introduces a range of learner motivations and goals. This leads to highly variable patterns of engagement both across MOOCs and often within the same MOOC. Conole (2013) suggests that participation can range from completely informal, with learners having the autonomy and flexibility to determine and chart their own learning journey, to engagement in a formal course, which operates in a similar manner to offline formal education. Furthermore, the curriculum and content of a MOOC is not always static, but incorporates (both by design and through differing modes of learner engagement) a range of learning opportunities and pathways, which individual learners are able to self-select and independently navigate. In contrast to the relatively linear, pre-established standards of traditional education, MOOCs enable individual learners to determine their engagement in relation to their self-identified goals (DeBoer et al. 2014).

However, as will be explored in greater detail later in this chapter, the agency that the term 'learner' endows can be problematic. Frequently, there is a disjunction between the espoused and enacted position of the learner. That is, not all learners in the MOOCs have the necessary knowledge, skills or dispositions to be an active agent in their learning journey and consequently cannot engage in the opportunities on offer in the same ways or for the same outcomes (Littlejohn et al. 2016). Equality of access does not result in equal outcomes across learners.

While the term learner (and the structure of MOOCs), in theory, but frequently not in practice, endows an individual with the agency to determine and chart their own learning journey, Biesta (2009) warns that the term learner also denotes a lack. That is, the learner is missing something that they must learn. The learner, therefore, is in a position of inequality, until they have learned whatever it is that they need to learn. In many ways, the positioning of MOOCs within the rhetoric of lifelong learning and the continuous need to upskill reinforces the learner as deficient in someway.

MOOCs increasingly are targeting this deficit in individuals and positioning themselves as the cure and solution to it. Later in this chapter, in the section on 'A closer look at the role of self-regulated learning in MOOCs', the implications for individual learners of this deficit thinking combined with the agency and self-directed nature of the learning experience in MOOCs will be explored in greater detail.

3.2.2 The User, the Participant

'User' is a term frequently used in discussions of technology. The meaning attached to the expression 'user' is mutable. In certain contexts, it refers to people 'using' content resources, which in the context of MOOCs serves to emphasise the notion of the MOOC as a product and learning as a commodity. This commoditisation of learning plays into the neoliberal position of education. In certain contexts, user may be used to convey freedom and agency to engage in the ways that best suit the individual. In this sense, it references the democratising power of technology, which can facilitate bottom-up activity by endowing individual users with the opportunity and ability to engage, lead and construct their online activity. The user, in conjunction with the educator or course developer, plays an integral role in the development and continued innovation and evolution of a particular product or experience. However, it equally may signify a closed and mechanistic use of the resources provided.

The term 'participant' serves to position the individual in an active role, and makes implicit reference to the centrality of technology to the experience. As such, they align with Siemens (2013) conception of the MOOC as a platform (rather than a course), on which individual learners (or users or participants) define and construct their own learning. Siemen's vision elevates a constructivist model of learning and knowledge over the transmission model in MOOCs. Thus, on a MOOC platform, users can be defined as—People who are offered rights to create, add, modify and disseminate content and knowledge through their interaction with other users and technology.

However, while the terms 'user' and 'participant' indicate a shared approach to learning where power and agency is distributed amongst all people involved in a MOOC, regardless of their position as convener or creator and learner, the reality of engagement in 'connectivist' learning environment (often referred to as cMOOCs, see Chap. 1) is more complex. While the terms 'user' and 'participant' (on the surface at least) afford agency to the individual actively to chart and determine the nature of their engagement, providing an allusion of user-control, the reality is somewhat different. Chapter 2 illustrated that cMOOCs, far from opening up education and the nature of engagement, require people to behave in specific ways. They are founded on everyone actively sharing and building knowledge, with each user or participant responsible for the continual evolution of the MOOC (Knox 2016). As such, they do not allow individuals to determine their own level of engagement. Passivity in a cMOOC is equated with non-engagement and nonconformity to the 'norms' of behaviour and learning (Milligan et al. 2013).

Yet the shifting language—student to learner, user to participant—suggests a reorienting of power in education and learning, with individual learners or participants responsible for identifying their learning needs and the learning opportunities that will be serve these. These individuals then moderate their behaviour and actions in order to reach their self-determined goals and outcomes. This shift in power is matched by a shifting of the role of learners. Ideally in a MOOC, every learner should simultaneously exist as a teacher by contributing their unique skills and knowledge back into the MOOC. However, many MOOC learners choose to learn individually and in isolation and few take responsibility for teaching others (Hew and Cheung 2014; Milligan et al. 2013), which means that the reality is somewhat different to the scenario suggested by the shift in terminology.

Feinberg (2001, p. 403) warns about this shift in power and emphasis on individual learners determining their learning needs. According to Feinberg, the expert knows best and the novice cannot make the decision about the pathway:

> In market models consumers are supposed to know what they need, and producers bid in price and quality to satisfy them. In professional models the producer not only services a need, but also defines it /…/ Sam goes to his physician complaining of a headache. Is it an aspirin or brain surgery that he needs? Only the doctor knows.

Social learning is an important characteristic of MOOCs. However, the plurality of the terminologies used to denote those who participate in MOOCs is symbolic of a shift away from 'the social' towards the 'individual'. Students are now termed learners and users are viewed as participants, symbolising the shift from what we perceive as 'education' to what we understand as 'learning'. This shift elevates and emphasises the position of the individual and individual pursuits. Whereas education is part of a broader programme, the aims and purposes of which we may or may not support. Through this agenda, students are members of an institutional structure and their socialisation within this structure becomes a pivotal part of their learning experience. Yet, the MOOC often becomes a decontextualised space, where the individual and the individual experience is emphasised.

3.3 Why a MOOC? Motivations and Incentives Among MOOC Learners

The democratising rhetoric surrounding MOOCs is acknowledged by Biesta (2009), who suggests that '[t]here are even emancipatory possibilities in the new language of learning to the extent to which it can empower individuals to take control of their own educational agendas' (p. 38). While the language empowers, the reality is that many learners do not have the cognitive, behavioural or affective characteristics necessary to be active agents and determiners of their own learning pathways. Early critiques of MOOCs suggested that they were not achieving their emancipatory aims but rather were reinforcing existing trends and inequalities in participation in education and learning. While this concern remains, there is growing evidence to suggest that MOOCs are attracting a broader demography of learners, and that learners have a broad range of motivations for engaging in a MOOC.

The open, flexible nature of MOOCs in theory—though not always in practice—enables individuals to determine with what, how and when they will engage. As a result, learners in MOOCs typically have a wider range of motivations and needs for learning than is normally observed in a conventional course or traditional educational experience. The flexible structure of MOOCs, in which there are few barriers and minimal formal consequences to learners 'dropping in' and 'dropping out' of a MOOC, leads to fluidity in learners' behaviours and actions (Yang et al. 2013).

The structure of learning in MOOCs, which typically involves minimal direct interaction between the instructor and learners, places the onus on each individual learner to determine and direct his or her own learning and to become teachers for other learners. Learners are not only required to self-regulate their learning, and to determine when, how and with what content and activities they engage, but they further have autonomy over determining the outcomes of their learning. The 'product' of a MOOC is not standardised across all learners. Learners can set some of their own terms of participation in MOOCs and therefore have a very different relationship to

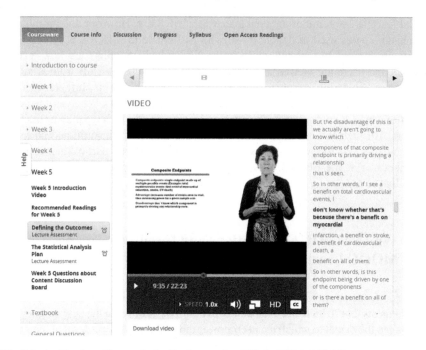

Fig. 3.1 A video-based lecture in the Fundamentals of Clinical Trials MOOC

course requirements, learning processes, and often the institution offering the MOOC compared with what occurs in traditional forms of higher education.

Research suggests that there is considerable variety in learners' motivations for enrolling in a MOOC (Littlejohn et al. 2016). Our own research on self-regulation in MOOCs suggests that learners displaying higher levels of self-regulation were more likely to conceptualise MOOCs as non-formal learning opportunities and to independently structure their learning and engagement to best serve their self-defined and self-identified needs (ibid.).

The Fundamentals of Clinical Trials MOOC (https://www.edX.org/course/ harvard-university/hsph-hms214x/fundamentals-clinical-trials/941) was run by the Harvard University over 12 weeks in 2013 using the edX platform. The course attracted 22,000 learners from 168 countries. The course was designed around a weekly rostrum, with regular, video-based lectures, as illustrated in Fig. 3.1.

Aside the video lectures, learners had access to other forms of course content including e-texts (Fig. 3.2).

Learners could interact through an online forum on the edX platform (Fig. 3.3) and assessments were computer marked (Fig. 3.4).

A study of the ways learners self-regulate their learning in this MOOC has previously been published (Milligan and Littlejohn 2016) and was compared with approaches to learning in the Introduction to DataScience MOOC, described in Chap. 4.

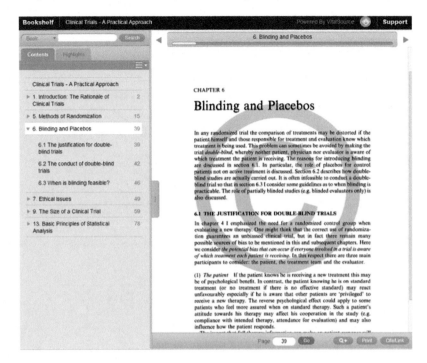

Fig. 3.2 An e-text from the Fundamentals of Clinical Trials MOOC

A study of the ways learners self-regulate their learning in this Fundamentals of Clinical Trials MOOC was compared with approaches to learning in the Introduction to Darascience MOOC described in Chap. 4. Self-regulation is a fluid characteristic that changes for each learner, depending on the context. Learners may be highly self-regulated in one context and less self-regulated in another. Thirty five learners, who perceived themselves as either a low or a high self-regulator, were interviewed.

Most learners who perceived themselves as poor self-regulators aimed to complete the MOOC and be awarded the course certificate:

> This class motivated me to do whatever was required to get the certificate … When I first took the course I thought I would use the course certificate … to add to my LinkedIn profile. I did do that. (LSRL, 783)

By contrast, learners who perceived themselves as highly self-regulated learners reported they were interested in the MOOC because it could improve their work performance:

> The most important factor… is not even how much I learn, but how big the impact of my work can be to the outside world. (HSRL, 119)

These motivations appeared to influence the learner's actions, in particular how they self-evaluated their learning and how satisfied they were with their progress. The high

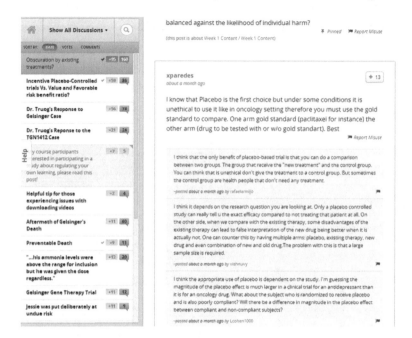

Fig. 3.3 Fundamentals of Clinical Trials MOOC online forum

self-regulators who participated in the MOOC to improve their work performance were strategic about where they focused their time and effort. When asked about whether and how they followed the course pathway, high self-regulators responded:

> [I tend to] follow what interests me and not worry too much about trying to keep a complete overview of the area… I plan to complete all of the assignments[but] I won't be too worried if I don't. (HSRL, 428)

> Carefully curated parts… I'm going to be picking through what nuggets are of use to me in particular contexts. (HSRL, 505)

However, learners who reported low self-regulation usually opted to follow the course pathway, spending time on the course materials:

> My goal is definitely to watch all the videos and the content provided and try to solve all the assignments, although not necessarily I will try to take part in the additional optional assignments. (LSRL, 603)

These learners tended to carry out most of the MOOC activities, in contrast to the high self-regulators who were more strategic about where they focus effort. More time was spent observing course materials, leading to difficulties with time management, compared with high self-regulators.

Another advantage for high self-regulators was that, because they set their own learning goals, they evaluated themselves against their own personal aims and were more able to self-assess their progress. There was evidence that high self-regulators

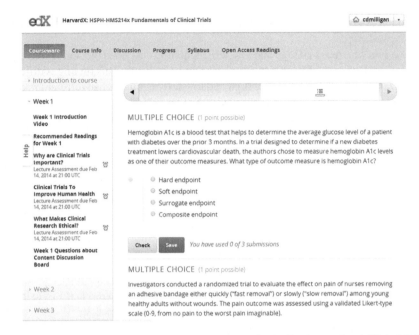

Fig. 3.4 Computer marked, multiple choice assessment in the Fundamentals of Clinical Trials MOOC

were self-satisfied with their progress, since they were readily able to identify their own learning gains. This relationship between perceived progress and affective power was explained as follows:

> Now I'm feeling more powerful, I can do some things, I am confident in finding solutions for problems that are too big for me right now. (HSRL, 670)

However, learners reporting low self-regulation experienced difficulty in self-evaluating their progress. This is because these learners tended to follow the course pathway and tried to self-evaluate their progress in relation to what was expected of them by the course designers, which was difficult for them to estimate. When questioned about self-evaluation, two respondents reported:

> It's hard for me to gauge how much I've understood something… sometimes we have a blindness about it ourselves. (LSRL, 236)

> Yeah that's a difficult question because I don't perceive my own learning. (LSRL, 396)

The second MOOC was Fundamentals of Clinical Trials, one of the first Harvard University MOOCs. The course was developed by the Harvard Medical School, Harvard School of Public Health and Harvard Catalyst and ran on the edX platform from November 2013 until April 2014 with 24,000 registered learners from around the world. The research design used the same method and instruments as used in the Introduction to Data Science study and has been previously reported (Milligan and

Littlejohn 2016). Thirty learners located in various countries around the world were interviewed.

Learners who reported high and low self-regulation described the same motivation for participating in the MOOC: to gain a Harvard certificate. This finding is different to the Data Science MOOC, where high and low self-regulators had different reasons for joining the MOOC. The reason why there is a difference in this MOOC is not clear, though gaining certification for professional development is more prevalent in the health sciences than in data science. Another reason could be because of the perceived value of a Harvard certificate.

However, even though high and low self-regulators had the same motivation for participating in the MOOC, their approach to goal-setting and learning strategies was different. Low self-regulators tended to follow the course 'pathway' set out by the instructional designers:

> I do download the study material which is provided by the course website, but while I watch the video I do not have a habit of making notes and I am a person who is organised in a mess. So even if I make a note I don't recollect and read those notes. (LSRL, 295)

> I've tried to go through the questions first and then go back and review the text to see…and that forces me to kind of focus on the topics a little bit more as opposed to if I go to the lecture and then try to do the questions I find myself zoning out during it. (LSRL, 360)

This behaviour is similar to the conduct of low self-regulators in the Introduction to Data Science MOOC.

Learners who reported high self-regulation also reported behaviours comparable with high self-regulators in the Data Science MOOC. These learners were strategic about their learning task strategies and time management:

> I don't put too much effort into what I'm learning, but this course – looking at the videos I get to take my time to understand. Sometimes I watch the video twice, which has really helped me to have a better understanding when I'm learning. (HSRL, 284)

These data illustrate that high self-regulators strategically manage their time and tasks. They select and engage in sections of a MOOC that support them meet their own goals, whether to attain a course certificate or to learn specific concepts or skills that they perceive as important. These learners may not appear to be engaged to learning, yet they intentionally are being selective about what they learn.

Common factors that motivated students to learn include: interest in the topic, access to free learning opportunities, the desire to update knowledge or to advance professionally, the opportunity to engage with world-class university content and the wish to gain accreditation and new credentials (Davis et al. 2014; Wintrup et al. 2015). Christensen et al. (2013) found that nearly half of MOOC students reported their primary reason for enrolling in a course was 'curiosity, just for fun', while 43.9% cited the opportunity to 'gain skills to do my job better'. While early engagers with MOOCs were more likely to be interest-driven, and so-called 'lifelong learners' whose incentives tended to be more heavily weighted towards intrinsic or internal factors, there is evidence that MOOCs increasingly are targeting the lucrative professional development market (Grossman 2013). They are learning for different reasons, compared with undergraduates or 'leisure learners', and will be attracted by differed sorts of incentives, such as learning specific knowledge to improve performance at work or gaining a qualification.

MOOC platform providers and universities are introducing new incentive structures which mimic those commonly found in traditional education. For example, credentialing is increasingly common among MOOC providers and courses that provide some form of credential or institutional accreditation are the highest growth areas (Shah 2016). In Chap. 1, we outlined how Coursera and Udacity have launched their own credentials, offering what Forbes Magazine has termed a 'badged-future', where accreditation is much more dynamic than in conventional education (see https://www.forbes.com/sites/ryancraig/2015/09/30/coursera-udacity-and-the-future-of-credentials/#300a92202b31).

There are other dramatic changes to education triggered by MOOCs. In a move, which Shah (2016) has termed MOOCs as a 'Netflix-like experience', a number of providers have responded to a demand from learners to have greater flexibility in when and how they engage in a MOOC by moving from courses being offered at set times during a year, to becoming self-paced and available continuously. This frees the learner from having to start a course on a date determined by an institution to beginning learning at a time that is convenient for them.

Mak et al. (2010, p. 280) suggestion that understanding learning in MOOCs requires a 'nuanced, strategic, dynamic and contextual' understanding of individual learners and individual MOOCs is remarkably apt. While there are lots of new benefits on offer, it is not always clear how these help [all of] the learners.

3.4 But Who Benefits?

In a MOOC, learners are able to set their own terms of participation, which is different from much of education where course objectives and learning designs are set. MOOC learners have a very different relationship to course requirements, learning processes even the institution offering the MOOC, compared with what occurs in traditional forms of higher education. Biesta (2009) explains this in relation to the new language of learning:

> The absence of explicit attention for the aims and ends of education is the effect of often implicit reliance on a particular 'common sense' view of what education is for. We have to bear in mind, however, that what appears as 'common sense' often serves the interests of some groups (much) better than those of others. (p. 37)

Indeed, we are witnessing that the design of MOOCs, the focus on the individual as the primary unit, and the emphasis on the individual as active agent in their learning journey, is privileging those who can learn. Self-regulation, therefore, emerges as a key lens for understanding nature of who is able to benefit from the learning opportunities offered in a MOOC. The wider context of a learner (rather than the often-superficial dimensions of prior educational attainment, geographic region, job) influences what they will get out of their learning journey. Selwyn labels this 'inequalities of participation' (2016, p. 31). That is, the experiences and outcomes of a particular learning experience will differ considerably, depending on who the person is.

Selwyn (2016) goes on to explain how a focus on equality of access without corresponding understanding of the need to ensure equality of participation has led to:

> The assumption that all individuals can navigate their own pathways through digital education opportunities implies a corresponding withdrawal of expert direction, guidance and support. While offering an alternative to the perceived paternalism of organised education provision, this approach does bump up against the widely held belief in education that learning is a social endeavour that is best supported by more knowledgeable others. (p. 74)

Cottom (2014) argues that online systems get designed and configured to 'the norm' of a self-motivated, highly able individual who is 'disembodied from place, culture, history, markets and inequality regimes'. That is, MOOCs tend to cater for those who have the social and educational capital to engage with the learning opportunities presented and furthermore, as briefly discussed in Chap. 1, MOOCs typically disregard the offline context of the learner and how this might influence and shape both the nature of their engagement and the outcomes they desire from their participation.

Without additional incentives, adults will not learn something that they are not interested in or consider unimportant (Billett and Somerville 2004; Illeris 2007; Siemens 2006). The choice to seek out and engage with both formal and informal learning opportunities and the proclivity and ability to adopt and assimilate new knowledge are determined by the individual. The experiences and interactions that have occurred throughout a person's life shape the values, beliefs, concepts and approach that they bring to their future learning (Rogoff 1990; Scribner 1985). A learner's personal ontogeny mediates and is mediated by the contexts in which they are situated and the orientation of their needs in relation to a particular learning opportunity. Individuals actively seek out opportunities that they believe will gratify the particular needs they have. The more gratification they receive, or expect to receive, from their actions, the more they will continue to engage in the behaviour. Conversely, negative outcome expectations lead to decreased engagement (LaRose et al. 2001; LaRose and Eastin 2004). A theme that recurs in this book is that disengagement is perceived as a significant problem in MOOCs, because few learners complete courses relative to formal education. (Jordan 2015). However, the emancipatory effect of free online access to education allows learner to take what they need from MOOCs to meet their own learning goals without formally completing courses, therefore completion rates can be misleading (LeBar 2014; Littlejohn and Milligan 2015).

In Chap. 1, we explored the spectrum of instructional designs applied to MOOCs. MOOC designs range from well-packaged content to open, networked designs. A problem with almost all MOOCs, no matter how they are designed, is that they tend not provide expert human feedback to learners, which means that the learners have to pursue advice and criticism themselves (Margaryan et al. 2015). This focus on the individual taking responsibility for their own feedback and learning journey means that those who benefit from MOOCs are the people who are best able to regulate their own learning. As McCathy (2011) explains:

> These discourses position the individuals as the locus of success or failure: based on their self-discipline, hard-work, ambition, personality and efforts, they will either fail or succeed procuring for their well-being .... Missing in these discourses is any consideration of the differential and inequitable positions of subjects in terms of economic, social and cultural capital, age, gender, class, race, ethnicity and sexual orientation. These discourses are based in the assumption that all subjects are equally positioned to identify, mobilize, and create productive and successful choices. (p. 303)

The next section examines how MOOC learners self-regulate their learning in MOOCs.

3.5 A Closer Look at the Role of Self-regulated Learning in MOOCs

Self-regulated learning provides a theoretical means for accommodating the diversity in motivations and incentives among learners and the mutable, learner-driven nature of the learning experience in MOOCs. Self-regulated learning refers to 'self-generated thoughts, feelings, and actions that are planned and cyclically adapted to the attainment of personal goals' (Zimmerman 2000, p. 14). In studies of formal, offline learning contexts, Zimmerman (1990) suggests that motivation and learning are interdependent processes and that individuals exhibiting higher self-regulation are more proactive in their approach to learning.

Similar findings have been observed in studies of MOOC learners. Those learners identified as exhibiting highly self-regulating behaviour were less concerned about outward measures of performance in MOOCs, preferring to concentrate on developing knowledge and expertise that was relevant to their professional needs (Littlejohn et al. 2016). That is, high self-regulators were more inclined to determine their own outcome measures rather than to rely on externally determined goals or incentive structures to shape their engagement. This contrasted to learners who exhibited lower self-regulated learning behaviours whose goals were more likely to be tied to concrete, traditional and extrinsic measures of performance, for example, completing all the assignments and earning a certificate of completion.

These findings align with research focused on offline learning which determined that learners displaying high self-regulative behaviour are more likely to adopt 'mastery goal orientation', structuring their learning around the development of content knowledge and expertise (Zimmerman 1990). Pintrich and de Groot (1990) similarly found that learners who considered their learning to be interesting and important are more cognitively engaged than those learners who are motivated primarily by grades. In research on MOOCs, those learners displaying higher levels of self-regulation were more likely to conceptualise MOOCs as non-formal learning opportunities and to independently structure their learning and engagement to best serve their self-defined and self-identified needs. The motivations a learner brings to a particular MOOC, together with the incentives structuring their engagement influences how they interpret the role and purpose of the MOOC and the outcomes they seek, which in turn shapes their behaviour and actions in the MOOC. As Illeris (2007) suggests, incentives influence the ways in which learners engage with or acquire content. As the following section will explore, this is not a monodirectional relationship. Content and the pedagogical design of a MOOC also influences the acquisition process.

3.6 Learning Behaviour: Diversity in Engagement

While MOOCs emphasise the primacy of the learner and the role individual learners' play in structuring their engagement, there has been a tendency in the literature on MOOCs to focus on design solutions that encourage desired modes of engagement and participation (see for example Guàrdia et al. 2013; Daradoumis et al. 2013). These desired learning behaviours borrow heavily on metrics derived from traditional forms of education. That is, the ideal learner is one who adopts behaviours that lead to the successful completion of a course and, where applicable, certification and accreditation. Traditional measures of learning, such as passing tests and assignments, and becoming accredited, continue to be the gold standard of successful learning in MOOCs. So much so that many researchers, when exploring the impact of different modes of engagement on a MOOC, continue to use completion as the dependent variable. There is a debate in the literature to 'reboot' research on how people learn in MOOCs by finding better indicators of learning in MOOCs (see Reich 2015).

Kizilcec et al. (2013) have developed a now widely accepted typology of four profiles of learner engagement in MOOCs: (i) auditing—learners who did not do the quizzes or assignments but engaged with other resources, such as the video lectures; (ii) completing—learners who completed all of the activities; (iii) disengaging—learners who participated at the beginning of a MOOC but whose engagement dropped off or ceased over time; and (iv) sampling—learners who engaged in resources once or twice, often in the middle of the course, but were not consistent in their engagement. While there have been some attempts in the literature to suggest that certain engagement profiles are 'better' than others, and indicative of greater learning, there is limited evidence to back this up. Ideas around 'good engagement' tend to be based on the assumption that MOOC learners intend to complete courses, akin to students in formal education courses (LeBar 2014). As we previously indicated, MOOCs allows learner to learn what they need from the course and drop out (Jordan 2015). MOOCs, therefore, have the potential to legitimise learning behaviour that in traditional contexts would be characterised as deviant, non-learning, associated with failure.

There are a number of typologies of MOOC learners and each takes a different perspective. For example, Milligan et al. (2013) identify different learning behaviours in MOOCs; Clow (2013) defines learners according to their participation; Gillani and Eynon (2014) define learners based on their engagement in discussion forums. None of these typologies examine learner engagement, even though taking part in MOOC a is a characteristic of MOOCs and is distinct from participation in formal education. We conclude this chapter with the construction of a new framework for understanding and interpreting learning engagement. This framework, importantly, does not make any attempt to suggest that any one approach is better or worse than another. Similarly, it does not suggest that a learner will always conform to a single approach.

Visible:

A visible learner is one whose presence and activity within a MOOC makes them 'known' by other learners. This may include participation and interaction in the discussions, undertaking and where applicable completing tasks, assessments and undertaking the activities required for certification.

Invisible:

These learners tend to be largely passive in their engagement in a MOOC. That is, their presence and activity is not visible to other learners. They do not actively contribute to discussion forum; however, they may read the posts an activity commonly referred to as 'lurking'. They rarely undertake activities and generally are not attempting to complete the course in a traditional sense or to gain certification.

Formal/qualification oriented:

These are the learners who perceive MOOCs as a formal learning activity, tend to treat a MOOC more like a traditional style of learning activity or course. These learners are likely to be more concerned with accreditation and ensuring that they 'complete' the MOOC and are likely to structure their engagement to achieve this.

Informal/interest-oriented:

These learners are less likely to be concerned with 'completing' the MOOC and are more interested in acquiring the knowledge and skills in the MOOC without requiring the formal documentation that they have done so. They tend to be more independent in their approach to learning, and able to identify the types of activities that they need to complete to get the outcomes that they desire (mainly self-identified and self-defined).

These variables position MOOC engagement in four distinct ways, as illustrated in the typology in Fig. 3.5.

The four types of learners will be discussed in greater detail in Chap. 4, where we sketch out narratives of the experiences of MOOC learners. These narratives make clear the validity of a range of learning behaviours in MOOCs. As a precursor to the stories of actual learners in that chapter, the four types are briefly described below.

The 'conventional' learner is one who is motivated to complete the course and gain certification. These learners are sometimes referred to as 'ideal learners' because their behaviour fits with what MOOC designers and facilitators believe to be optimal and Eynon (2014) define learners based on their engagement in discussion forums. None of these typologies examine learner engagement, even though taking part in MOOC a is a characteristic of MOOCs and is distinct from participation in formal education. We conclude this chapter with the construction of a new framework for understanding and interpreting learning engagement. This framework, importantly, does not make any attempt to suggest that any one approach is better or worse than another. Similarly, it does not suggest that a learner will always conform to a single approach.

Visible:

A visible learner is one whose presence and activity within a MOOC makes them 'known' by other learners. This may include participation and interaction in the discussions, undertaking and where applicable completing tasks, assessments and undertaking the activities required for certification.

Invisible:

These learners tend to be largely passive in their engagement in a MOOC. That is, their presence and activity is not visible to other learners. They do not actively contribute to discussion forum; however, they may read the posts an activity commonly referred to as 'lurking'. They rarely undertake activities and generally are not attempting to complete the course in a traditional sense or to gain certification.

Formal/qualification oriented:

These are the learners who perceive MOOCs as a formal learning activity, tend to treat a MOOC more like a traditional style of learning activity or course. These learners are likely to be more concerned with accreditation and ensuring that they 'complete' the MOOC and are likely to structure their engagement to achieve this.

Informal/interest-oriented:

These learners are less likely to be concerned with 'completing' the MOOC and are more interested in acquiring the knowledge and skills in the MOOC without requiring the formal documentation that they have done so. They tend to be more independent in their approach to learning, and able to identify the types of activities that they need to complete to get the outcomes that they desire (mainly self-identified and self-defined).

These variables position MOOC engagement in four distinct ways, as illustrated in the typology in Fig. 3.5.

The four types of learners will be discussed in greater detail in Chap. 4, where we sketch out narratives of the experiences of MOOC learners. These narratives make clear the validity of a range of learning behaviours in MOOCs. As a precursor to the stories of actual learners in that chapter, the four types are briefly described below.

The 'conventional' learner is one who is motivated to complete the course and gain certification. These learners are sometimes referred to as 'ideal learners' because their behaviour fits with what MOOC designers and facilitators believe to be optimal

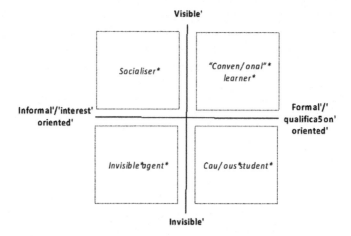

Fig. 3.5 A typology of MOOC Learners

for course completion (even though this behaviour may not fit with the learners' own objectives). They tend to follow a largely linear trajectory, engaging with the majority of the content and completing the activities and assessments. Furthermore, they are active contributors to the discussion forums, both asking and answering questions, and consider collaboration with other participants a key part of the MOOC experience.

The cautious student also has a goal to complete the course and as a result—similarly to the 'conventional' student—will engage with the majority of the course content and activities. However, they often are not as confident and at times struggle to regulate their learning and to select the best learning approaches for their needs. Furthermore, they typically are reticent to post to discussion forums, though they may read the contributions of others.

The invisible learner is motivated by a desire to learn, rather than to receive accreditation or to complete a course. They often are highly regulated and are able to carefully match their engagement to their needs and motivation. Their behaviour may perfectly fit their own learning objectives, but is not 'ideal' for the course facilitators or even for the other learners. They may be passive in their engagement and driven by a desire for content and skills. Consequently, they typically do not undertake the activities or assessments and do not contribute to the discussion forums.

The socialiser, analogous to the invisible learner, is not motivated by a desire to complete the course or the prescribed activities. They similarly are able to chart their own engagement with confidence. They may undertake some activities. However, their preliminary focus is collaborating with other participants, by contributing to the discussion forums.

MOOC participants tend to align with these learner types, depending on their motivations, and may span different types, rather than falling into one single category.

3.7 Concluding Thoughts

The rhetoric around MOOCs has stressed their democratising potential, creating a vision of the emancipated learner, who is no longer reliant on traditional institutions and the barriers—financial, geographic, admission requirements—that they can pose. While the language frequently employed suggests a reorienting of power in education and learning, and elevating the role of the individual learner, it belies the responsibility that comes with this new role. As this chapter has shown, the learners in MOOCs are incredibly heterogeneous, with diverse motivations, goals and learning needs. The four learner types discussed in this chapter will be explored in greater detail in Chap. 4, as well examine the diverse ways in which massive numbers of people learn in MOOCs.

Acknowledgements The authors wish to thank Vasudha Chaudhari of The Open University for comments and for proofing this chapter.

References

Biesta, G. (2009). Good education in an age of measurement: On the need to reconnect with the question of purpose in education. *Education Assessment Evaluation Association, 21*, 33–46.

Billett, S., & Somerville, M. (2004). Transformation at work: Identity and learning. *Studies in Continuing Education, 26*(2), 309–326.

Christensen, G., Steinmetz, A., Alcorn, B., Bennett, A., Woods, D., & Emanuel, E. J. (2013). The MOOC phenomenon: Who takes Massive Open Online Courses and why? Available from: http://ssrn.com/abstract=2350964.

Clow, D. (2013, April). MOOCs and the funnel of participation. In *Proceedings of the Third International Conference on Learning Analytics and Knowledge* (pp. 185–189). ACM.

Conole, G. (2013). MOOCs as disruptive technologies: Strategies for enhancing the learner experience and quality of MOOCs. *RED - Revista de Educación a Distancia, 39*. Available from: http://www.um.es/ead/red/39/conole.pdf.

Cottom, T. (2014). Democratising ideologies and inequality regimes. Cambridge, MA: Berkman Centre for Internet & Society Series, Harvard University.

Daradoumis, T., Bassi, R., Xhafa, F., & Caballé, S. (2013, October). A review on massive e-learning (MOOC) design, delivery and assessment. In *2013 Eighth International Conference on P2P, Parallel, Grid, Cloud and Internet Computing (3PGCIC)* (pp. 208–213). IEEE.

Davis, H., Dickens, K., Leon, M., del Mar Sanchez Ver, M., & White, S. (2014). MOOCs for Universities and Learners: An analysis of motivating factors. In: *6th International Conference on Computer Supported Education, 01–03 April 2014*.

DeBoer, J., Ho, A., Stump, G., & Breslow, L. (2014) Changing "course": reconceptualizing educational variables for massive open online courses. *Educational Researcher*, 1–11. https://doi.org/10.3102/0013189x14523038.

Feinberg, W. (2001). Choice, autonomy, need-definition and educational reform. *Studies in Philosophy of Education, 20*(5), 402–409.

Ferguson, R., & Sharples, M. (2014, September). Innovative pedagogy at massive scale: Teaching and learning in MOOCs. In *European Conference on Technology Enhanced Learning* (pp. 98–111). Cham: Springer.

Gillani, N., & Eynon, R. (2014). Communication patterns in massively open online courses. *The Internet and Higher Education, 23*, 18–26.

Grossman, R. J. (2013). Are massive open online courses in your future? *HR Magazine, 58*(8), 30–36.

Guàrdia, L., Maina, M., & Sangrà, A. (2013). MOOC design principles: A pedagogical approach from the learner's perspective. *eLearning Papers*, (33).

Hew, K. F., & Cheung, W. S. (2014). Students' and instructors' use of massive open online courses (MOOCs): Motivations and challenges. *Educational Research Review, 12*, 45–58.

Illeris, K. (2007). *How we learn: Learning and non-learning in School and Beyond*. London: Routledge.

Jordan, K. (2015). Massive open online course completion rates revisited: Assessment, length and attrition. *The International Review of Research in Open and Distributed Learning, 16*(3).

Kizilcec, R., Piech, C., & Schneider, E. (2013). Deconstructing disengagement: Analyzing learner subpopulations in massive open online courses. *LAK '13 Leuven, Belgium*.

Knox, J. (2016). *Posthumanism and the massive open online course: Contaminating the subject of global education*. Routledge.

LaRose, R., & Eastin, M. (2004). A social cognitive theory of internet uses and gratifications: Toward a new model of media attendance. *Journal of Broadcasting and Electronic Media, 48*(3), 358–377.

LaRose, R., Mastro, D., & Eastin, M. (2001). Understanding Internet usage: A social-cognitive approach to uses and gratifications. *Social Science Computer Review, 19*(4), 395–412.

LeBar, M. (2014) MOOCs—Completion is not important. *Forbes*. Available from August 20, 2017: http://www.forbes.com/sites/ccap/2014/09/16/moocs-finishing-is-not-the-important-part/.

Littlejohn, A., Hood, N., Milligan, C., & Mustain, P. (2016). Learning in MOOCs: Motivations and self-regulated learning in MOOCs. *The Internet and Higher Education, 29*, 40–48.

Littlejohn, A., & Milligan, C. (2015) Designing MOOCs for professional learners: Tools and patterns to encourage self-regulated learning, *eLearning Papers, 42*, Special Issue on Design Patterns for Open Online Teaching and Learning. Accessed August 20, 2017 from http://www.openeducationeuropa.eu/en/node/170924.

Mak, J., Williams, S., & Mackness, R. (2010). The ideals and reality of participating in a MOOC. In L. Dirckinck-Holmfeld, V. Hodgson, C. Jones, M. de Laat, D. McConnell, & T. Ryberg (Eds.), *Proceedings of the 7th International Conference on Networked Learning 2010*.

Margaryan, A., Bianco, M., & Littlejohn, A. (2015). Instructional quality of massive open online courses (MOOCs). *Computers & Education, 80*, 77–83.

McCathy, C. (2011). Afterword. In Peters and E. Bulut (Eds.), *Cognitive capitatlism, education and digital labour* (pp. 301–321). Berlin: Peter Lang.

Milligan, C., & Littlejohn, A. (2016). How health professionals regulate their learning in massive open online courses. *The Internet and Higher Education, 31*, 113–121.

Milligan, C., Margaryan, A., & Littlejohn, A. (2013). Patterns of engagement in connectivist MOOCs. *Journal of Online Learning and Teaching, 9*(2). http://jolt.merlot.org/vol9no2/milligan_0613.htm.

Pintrich, P., & de Groot, E. (1990). Motivational and self-regulated learning components of classroom academic performance. *Journal of Educational Psychology, 82*(1), 33–40.

Reich, J. (2015). Rebooting MOOC research. *Science, 347*(6217), 34–35.

Rensfeldt, A. (2012). (Information) technologies of the self: Personalisation as a new model of subjectivation and knowledge production. *E-Learning and Digital Media, 9*(4), 406–418.

Rogoff, B. (1990). *Apprenticeship in thinking: Cognitive development in social context*. Oxford and New York: Oxford University Press.

Scribner, S. (1985). Vygotsky's uses of history. In J. Wertsch (Ed.), *Culture, communication, and cognition: Vygotskian perspectives* (pp. 119–145). Cambridge: Cambridge University Press.

Selwyn, N. (2014). *Distrusting educational technology*. London and New York: Routledge.

Selwyn, N. (2016). *Is technology good for education*. Cambridge, UK: Polity Books.

Shah, D. (2016). By the numbers: MOOCS in 2016. [Online]. Retrieved from https://www.class-central.com/report/mooc-stats-2016/.

Siemens, G. (2006). Knowing knowledge. [Online]. Available from www.knowingknowledge.com.

Siemens, G. (2013). Massive open online courses: Innovation in education. *Open Educational Resources: Innovation, Research and Practice, 5,* 5–15.

Wintrup, J., Wakefield, K., & Davis, H. (2015). *Engaged learning in MOOCs: A study using a the UK engagement survey.* The Higher Education Academy.

Yang, D., Sinha, T., Adamson, D., & Rose, C. P. (2013). "Turn on, tune in, drop out": Anticipating student dropouts in massive open online courses. In: *Proceedings of the NIPS Workshop on Data Driven Education* (pp. 1–8). Retrieved from http://lytics.stanford.edu/datadriveneducation/papers/yangetal.pdf.

Zimmerman, B. (1990). Self-regulated learning and academic achievement: An overview. *Educational Psychologist, 25*(1), 3–17.

Zimmerman, B. (2000). Attaining self-regulation: A social cognitive perspective. In M. Boekaerts, M. Zeidner, & P. Pintrich (Eds.), *Handbook of self-regulation* (pp. 13–39). San Diego, CA: Academic Press.

Chapter 4
Massive Numbers, Diverse Learning

Abstract MOOCs provide education for millions of people worldwide. Though it is not clear whether everyone can learn in a MOOC. Building on the typology of MOOC participants introduced is in Chap. 3, and we explore the claim that MOOCs are for everyone. We trace the different reasons people participate in MOOCs and the ways they learn. MOOCs tend to be designed for people who are already able to learn as active, autonomous learners. Those with low confidence may be inactive. However, even learners who are confident and able to regulate their learning experience difficulties if they don't comply with the expectations of the course designers or their peers. For example, if a learner chooses to learn by observing others, rather than contributing, this behaviour can be perceived negatively by tutors and by peers. This indicates that MOOCs sustain the traditional hierarchy between the educators (those that create MOOCs and technology systems) and the learners (those who use these courses and systems). Although this hierarchy is not always visible, since it is embedded within the algorithms and analytics that power MOOC tools and platforms.

4.1 Learning in MOOCs; What Does It Mean?

MOOCs have massive number of learners with diverse intentions and characteristics. Yet, little is known about how and why they engage in MOOCs. Research on learning in MOOCs tends to focus on MOOC designs, the data trails of learners and the semantic traces they leave in discussion forums (Gasevic et al. 2014). These studies tell little about the cognitive and affective factors that influence the reasons that learners study, their learning strategies, why they drop in and out of courses and whether they have learnt. Few researchers examining learning in MOOCs have taken a holistic view of learners' experiences, for example, by gathering learners' stories and listening to them describe their motivations, experiences and feelings about learning in a MOOC. Yet an all-inclusive view is needed to allow critical analysis that positions learning and technology within broader organisational, political, economic and social contexts in order to explore how it can foster, support and counteract issues of empowerment, equality and democratisation (Selwyn 2010).

© The Author(s) 2018

A. Littlejohn and N. Hood, *Reconceptualising Learning in the Digital Age*,
SpringerBriefs in Open and Distance Education,
https://doi.org/10.1007/978-981-10-8893-3_4

This chapter is informed by a programme of research overseen by one of the authors which was based around conversations with 88 learners in three different MOOCs (see Littlejohn et al. 2016; Milligan and Littlejohn 2016; Milligan et al. 2013). This research was motivated by the claim that MOOCs are opening up education, which is underscored by the assumption that MOOC learners are able to self-regulate their own learning. Our findings questioned this claim, highlighting that MOOCs open up education principally for people who are already able to learn. Our findings contest the belief that MOOCs challenge existing models and paradigms of education. In fact our research illustrates that MOOCs are, in some ways, reinforcing traditional patterns and behaviours in both learning and learners. The pluralism that characterises the need for learners to be able to learn actively in MOOCs and the limited ability of many MOOC learners to self-regulate their learning makes any attempt to discuss MOOCs in a unified manner challenging. Furthermore, the absence of strong, extant theoretical frameworks for conceptualising learning in a digital age further limits the academic scholarship in this area.

Building on the typology of learners presented at the end of Chap. 3, this chapter re-examines the potential to reconceptualise learning and learners in MOOCs, while simultaneously questioning how much of this reconceptualisation is current reality, versus a desired future vision. The pluralism present in the structure and purpose of individual MOOCs is matched by the multiplicity of stances and approaches adopted in this chapter. While, to the academic purist, moving between different theoretical framings in a single chapter may be criticised, we argue that this multiple framing aligns perfectly with the diverse frameworks governing the approaches to learning in individual MOOCs and diversity of backgrounds, motivations and behaviours of MOOC learners.

MOOCs frequently are positioned as re-operationalising traditional concepts in education, representing a new approach to instruction and learning (Fischer 2014). In Chap. 2 we characterised how the MOOC platform providers, along with their university partners, have emphasised a re-orientation of learning through open access to courses that are free of charge, use learning materials created by elite faculty and facilitate interaction with thousands of other learners. At the same time, those who use the 'connectivist' approach to MOOCs argue that the idea of learning in an open and autonomous network changes the educational paradigm (Downes 2012). While this is undoubtedly true in some cases, the degree to which they are re-operationalising and reconceptualising the learning process requires careful consideration. MOOCs hold an uncertain space where they appear simultaneously to challenge traditional approaches and paradigms, while continuing to draw on and replicate existing educational and learning models.

To explore this tension between novelty and continuity in MOOCs, we draw upon Illeris' (2007) fundamental processes of learning framework as a lens for examining the nature of learning. More particularly learning framework can be used for considering the positioning of the individual learner in relation to their broader MOOC experience. Illeris suggests that at its most basic, learning requires two simultaneously occurring processes: (1) external interaction between the learner and their social, cultural and material environment(s), where their activities and actions are situated; and (2) the internal, psychological process of acquisition and elaboration, where new stimuli are connected with prior learning. These internal processes are mediated through the individual, arising from the interplay between the incentives influencing and structuring an individual's behaviour, and engagement with content and learning activities.

Put more simply, to understand any learning, it is necessary to consider how an individual learner draws upon his or her existing cognitive frameworks, personal ontologies and social capital to navigate the experiences, resources, tools and spaces made available to them. How is the learner and his or her learning activity situated within their broader contexts of action?

Illeris (2007) states all learning involves three dimensions: cognitive (knowledge and skills), affective (feelings and motivation) and social (communication and co-operation), which are embedded in the learning context (in this case the MOOC). Thus, Illeris' model combines the internal psychological stance of the individual, with the socially mediated dimensions of the learning process.

Therefore, to understand the nature of learning in MOOCs, it is necessary to consider how the internal drive to learn is transformed into learning opportunities through an individual's engagement with the socio-cultural and socio-technical contexts of practice. In these contexts learning is distributed across the individual, other people, resources, technology and physical contexts (Cobb and Bower 1999; Greeno et al. 1996; Pea 1997; Putnam and Borko 1997). Learning is embedded within the individual's cognition, influenced and shaped by their personal histories, as well as situated in the environmental, social and technological contexts in which the individual operates. Learning is explored through individual learners' interactions with online systems, with other people and with (online and offline) information resources (Abeer and Miri 2014). Therefore, learners are influenced by their own cognition and experiences, their social surroundings and both the digital and physical contexts in which the learning is embedded.

Eraut (1994) suggests that learning does not occur when an individual encounters an idea or information, but rather through new input or use. It is through being enacted that an idea gets reinterpreted and acquires new meaning, which is specific to the individual and their context. This moves beyond the learning as acquisition metaphor (Hakkarainen and Paavola 2007; Sfard 1998) to the conceptualisation of learning as construction (Piaget 1964). Hakkarainen and Paavola (2007) suggest that in this conception:

> Learning is seen as analogous to innovative inquiry through which new ideas, tools and practices to support intelligent action are created and the knowledge being developed is significantly enriched or changed during the process.

Learning, therefore, occurs within the internal, psychological setting of the individual (thinking) as well as through the actions of an individual, (behaviour), which are situated within a particular environmental context (Illeris 2007).

This reading of learning in MOOCs is in contrast to much of the literature, which characterises MOOCs as de-contextualised learning experiences. MOOC platform providers view MOOCs as contained courses supported by distributed and fragmented technology tools, rather than as a holistic learning journey that brings together all the experiences and contexts each individual learner engages within (Ebben and Murphy 2014). To more fully understand the nature of the learning experience it is necessary to situate the MOOC, the learning opportunities it provides, and individual learners within the multiple ecosystems in which they interact.

From this perspective, learning is not prescriptive or predefined by a set of objectives. While the curriculum and learning outcomes of a particular MOOC may guide the discourse and activities of the learners, the specific knowledge and concepts that are learnt will emerge through the activities and actions of the learners, and will, therefore, be influenced by a myriad of factors (Milligan et al. 2013; Williams et al. 2011). These factors encompass the understanding and experience the learner brings to the course, including their motivation and level of confidence, the knowledge of other learners, the course design, and the temporal and geographic contexts in which the MOOC and its learners are situated.

4.2 Individual-Level Factors

A number of studies have sought to identify the individual-level factors that influence successful learning in MOOCs. A learner's geographic location affects not only accessibility to MOOCs, but also their interest in topics (Liyanagunawardena et al. 2013), with demographic information positioned as a mediating factor to explain behaviour in a MOOC (Skrypnyk et al. 2015). Confidence, prior experience and motivation (Littlejohn et al. 2016; Milligan et al. 2013), and a learner's occupation (de Waard et al. 2011; Hood et al. 2015; Wang and Baker 2015) further have been found to mediate engagement. A relationship between learners' goals and their learning outcomes has also been identified (Kop et al. 2011; Littlejohn et al. 2016), while there is also evidence that a learners' prior education experience influence their retention in a MOOC (Emanuel 2013; Koller et al. 2013; Rayyan et al. 2013).

Some of these individual-level factors identified in the literature are associated with the norms and expectations of how learners behave in education. Other factors, raised in Chap. 3, are focused around the role of motivations, incentives and self-regulation in determining how a learner engages within the learning environment.

4.3 The Environment

Learning is enabled in part through an individual's participation within their context of practice, as well as through interaction and engagement with the resources (material and human) available in that context (Lave and Wenger 1991). The learning process and resultant knowledge is shaped by the context(s) in which knowledge is acquired and used. Nonaka and Toyama (2003) utilise the concept of *ba*, to explain the specific context, encompassing both spatial and temporal dimensions, in which learning takes place and knowledge is created. *Ba* is a shared space for emerging relationships composed of physical (classroom, office, etc.), virtual (digital tools, platforms) and mental (concepts, ideas, shared knowledge) dimensions.

The environment is not a single, static entity but rather is comprised of multiple complex systems, which come together to inform and shape the ways in which a learner engages with learning opportunities and resources. Barron (2006), in her work on learning ecologies, describes the importance of understanding the multiple environments in which technology-enabled learning occurs:

> Understanding how learning to use technology is distributed among multiple settings and resources is an increasingly important goal. The questions of how, when, and why adolescents choose to learn are particularly salient now, as there has been a rapid increase in access to information and to novel kinds of technologically mediated learning environments such as online special interest groups, tutorials, or games.
>
> It has become easier for those with computer access to find resources and activities that can support their learning in their own terms. However, there are also widespread concerns about equity. Although physical access to computing tools is becoming less of an issue, there are still stark differences among children and adolescents in access to learning opportunities that will help position them to use computers in ways that can promote their own development. In addition, there is the related concern that we convince a more diverse set of people to pursue advanced knowledge that will position them to work in technological design fields. (p. 194)

Barron goes on to explain that:

> The survey responses indicated that often learning was distributed over several settings and across many types of resources. More experienced students accessed a greater number of resources both in and out of school. Individual differences in the range and types of learning resources utilized were found even when physical access to computers and to the Internet were the same, suggesting that differences were due to variations in interest or resourcefulness. The results also suggested critical interdependencies between contexts. (2006, p. 196).

Therefore, to fully understand the learning that occurs in a MOOC it is necessary to understand both the individual learner, as well as how the learner is situated in and navigates the multiple spaces, contexts and settings in which they and their learning are situated and the materials and resources on which they draw.

4.4 Analysing the Norms of Behaviour

As Chap. 3 investigated, identifying a single 'norm' of behaviour or type of engagement in a MOOC is impossible. MOOCs, at least in theory, are positioned to endow learners with the flexibility to determine and chart their own individual learning journeys. Consequently, learning cannot be understood without deep engagement with the experiences of individual learners. That is, learning is inseparable from the personal histories and experiences, beliefs, and motivations of individual learners as well as their broader socio-cultural context and the relationship between the MOOC and their offline contexts. It is difficult to know whether someone has learned unless all of these factors are taken into account. Narrative accounts of learning provide the sorts of qualitative data needed to understand whether a learner is learning. However, these data are difficult to analyse and draw conclusions from.

To get around this problem and simplify analyses of learning in MOOCs, there has been an emphasis on identifying digital trace data that can be analysed to monitor academic performance. The greater the number of learners who provide data, the larger the potential to analyse data in meaningful ways and provide scaffolds and supports for learners.

Learning analytics usually is designed around one or more of the following:

- *early alert systems* that predict the likelihood of a learner falling behind or dropping out of a course;
- *visualisation systems* that provide dashboards to tutors and learners illustrating progress in relation to a pathway pre-prescribed by the tutor or in relation to the learner's position within a network of peers and tutors;
- *recommender systems* that endorse resources, people or future pathways;
- *adaptive learning systems* that aim to personalize the resources, people or future pathways the learner accesses, depending on their demographics or progress.

Early alert systems are based on predictive analytics that predetermine the learner's likelihood of achieving a 'success' measure, by comparing the learner's data to those of other students. For example, systems have been developed to analyse contributions to discussion forums and use these data to predict the likelihood of a learner dropping out (Muñoz-Merino et al. 2015; Skrypnyk et al. 2015; Vu et al. 2015). Learners' engagement and progression in a MOOC has been linked with a learner's prior education level (Rayyan et al. 2013). Jiang et al (2014) found factors related to a learner's behaviour in week 1 of a MOOC to be early alert indicators that signal whether or not a student would complete the MOOC. These factors included the number of assessments completed by the learner and the score from quizzes within the MOOC. Other early alert indicators link time management in a MOOC and retention (Balakrishnan and Cooetzee 2013). Retention rates have been correlated with a lighter workload, higher autonomy and more flexible assessments; the highest levels of perseverance were connected to autonomy, high levels of learning support and scaffolding activities (Skrypnyk et al. 2015).

Visualisation systems include Social Network Analysis techniques that use the learner's position within a learning network as an indicator of his or her connectedness, assuming a relationship between the learner's position in a learning network associated with a MOOC and the likelihood of them leaving the course (Yang et al. 2014). The learner's position within this network may be strengthened through interactions with peers and tutors using social media tools such as blogging and microblogging tools or by linking with others through discussion threads (ibid.). Other visualisation methods combine learning characteristics data with cognitive and behavioural data. For example Buckingham–Shum and Deakin–Crick (2012) link data on student's ability to self-direct their learning with assessment data to feedback to learners how they might amend their learning in ways that allow them to achieve success. Other, similar systems use recommendations, for example advocating that learners with a similar profile took a specific course of action (e.g. reading a text or engaging in a supplementary course) to achieve success.

Recommender systems offer MOOC learners all kinds of guidance, including advice about the next MOOC they select, or the likelihood of successful completion of a course. These recommendations are based on different kinds of data gathered from the learner and analysed against previous data from earlier rounds of the course. For example Skrypnyk et al. (2015) reported how analysis of learners' demographics and cultural groupings allowed personalised recommendations to students about the actions they could take to scaffold their learning. Emerging analytics systems are gathering a wider range of data, including affective data that indicate how learners feel about their learning. These data allow for more influential recommendations and adaptations of learning resources.

Adaptable systems include MOOCs where content is tailored and personalised for each student (Tabba and Medouri 2013). Some techniques adapt the learning design of a course, depending on the data (Mor et al. 2015). Other systems use semantic analysis of online discussions in MOOCs to allow adaptation. Gillani et al. (2014) examined the strategies of hundreds of learners as they engaged in online discussions. Using complex network analysis techniques, they identified a number of 'significant interaction networks' embedded within discussion forums. Although these interaction networks can support learning, they are vulnerable to breaking down. MOOC providers are capitalising on these analytics techniques to structure discussion forums so that students who join the course late are as able as the early cohorts to form lasting bonds and get integrated into the cohort of students taking the course.

Earlier, we indicated that learning is inseparable from the learner's personal experiences, beliefs and motivations, but data around these factors is difficult to measure and analyse. As a shortcut measure, it is sometimes assumed that 'learning' is synonymous with active engagement in a MOOC and with retention, completion and certification (see, for example Hew 2014). An example is a study by Colvin et al. (2014) analysed learning in the 8.MReV Mechanics ReView MOOC, offered on the EdX platform from June to August 2013. The course, an introduction to Newtonian Mechanics, was run in parallel with an on-campus course at MIT. The MOOC version of the course substituted face-to-face lectures with video lectures and textbooks with digital texts, and was open to anyone who met a number of prerequisites. The course design was structured around weekly video lectures to help students engage with task-based problem. The learning gains of 1080 students were evaluated by analysing the results of pre- and post-tests through normalised gain and item response theory. The learning gains for these students were comparable with those in the on-campus class, and 95% achieved the MOOC certificate. However, unlike the campus-based course, most of the MOOC students (almost 16,000 of the 17,000 people registered for the MOOC) did not complete the course and achieve the certificate.

This example illustrates that as technology advances, MOOC providers need to rethink MOOC models, and the role that tracking can play in them. Gathering data is likely to be more streamlined into online learning and those data that are easiest to measure are often used more prominently in analyses. However, one issue to consider is whether the right data is being gathered (Gašević et al. 2015).

At times the application of analytics overlooks the fact that technology is socially constructed and negotiated, rather than imbued with predetermined characteristics (Gašević et al. 2015). Poor application of analytics may promote a narrow view of desired outcomes and norms of behaviour in a MOOC which belie the fluidity and flexibility of the learning opportunities that MOOCs can offer.

Over-reliance on learning analytics for understanding and measuring learning may lead to what Biesta (2009) has termed 'normative validity'. That is:

> The question whether we are indeed measuring what we value, or whether we are just measuring what we can easily measure and thus end up valuing what we [can] measure. (p. 35)

There is a danger that, by missing the learner's context, that analytics systems may oversimplify how we understand learning. There are three key problems. First systems may focus on data that are easily measured—retention, completion and certification, rather than what cannot be easily measured—learner motivations, goals, self-regulation and agency—but are nevertheless critically important to learning. Second, those who code the algorithms that underpin analytics may not be concerned with the wider questions of the learner's context and consequences for their learning decisions (Morozov 2014). The Joint Committee of the European Supervisory Authorities has undertaken a consultation on big data and the financial profiling of customers, emphasising that the algorithms that are used in big data analytics must be shown to be unbiased, otherwise the benefits of analysis will be diminished (ESA 2016).

While learning analytics provide the potential to personalise the learning experiences and opportunities of learners in MOOCs, the extent to which they can currently do this is questionable. Selwyn (2016) suggests that rather than personalising the learning experience, analytics instead is reinforcing mass customization of education through large systems. He explains:

> Many personalised, bespoke learning systems are concerned primarily with delivering predetermined content to students, albeit in different sequences and various forms of presentation. (p. 72)

Learning analytics in MOOCs may "personalise" the learning but this "personalisation" is not to the individual needs or goals of the learner but rather to the behavioural norms and desired outcomes of the MOOC provider. The learner's behaviours are being adjusted to maximise the outcomes for the course providers, rather than the learning being optimised to meet the learner's needs and objectives. This is because the assumptions that underpin the analytics may be based on the MOOC provider's requirements, rather than the learners's aspirations.

Algorithms are developed by coders to analyse data in a meaningful way. These can be helpful in understanding data, but inevitably are shaped by underpinning assumptions and biases. Data gathered and analysed by algorithms are limited by the expertise and assumptions held by those people who write the code (Williamson

2015). If the coders do not appreciate the underlying assumptions of their codes, then the data the algorithms analyse can be compromised. According to Boyd and Crawford (2011):

> As computational scientists have started engaging in acts of social science, there is a tendency to claim their work as the business of facts and not interpretation. A model may be mathematically sound, an experiment may seem valid, but as soon as a researcher seeks to understand what it means, the process of interpretation has begun. This is not to say that all interpretations are created equal, but rather that not all numbers are neutral.

Researchers such as Williamson (2015) warn that these biases may result in a hierarchy between those that create MOOC systems and those who use these courses and systems, such that empowered 'producers' of technical systems indirectly can overly influence and exploit the student consumers of the systems. To aim for equality, we need to engage with and interpret the qualitative narratives of individual MOOC learners.

4.5 Qualitative Narratives and Learners' Stories

> Inequalities persist even for those people who do get to take part. In particular, experiences and outcomes of education differ considerably according to who someone is – what is often referred to as 'inequalities of participation'. (Selwyn 2016, p. 31).

Engaging with the qualitative narratives of individual MOOC participants enables a richer perspective of what it means to learn in a MOOC. An example of a MOOC where we have gathered narratives of how learners have learned is *Introduction to Data Science* (https://www.coursera.org/course/datasci). This MOOC was offered in 2014 by the University of Washington on the Coursera platform. The course was designed for people with a moderate level of programming experience. Over 8 weeks, 50,000 learners, from 197 countries participated in the course.

The course homepage, illustrated in Fig. 4.1, provided information about the course aims and instructional design.

To achieve the course aims, learners were expected to engage in a number programming activities, supplemented by educational materials including video lectures (Fig. 4.2).

Learner interactions were enabled through sharing data science examples (see Fig. 4.3), uploading assignments, engaging in online discussions within the MOOC platform as well as collaboration through other social media sites, including OpenStack, an online site commonly used by computer scientists to share codes and discuss coding problems. Through creating and sharing computer codes, the learners independently structured informal learning and combined this with the formal learning activities within the MOOC. This ability to personalise learning outcomes was important for professional learners who wanted to align their learning in the MOOC with their job.

2015). If the coders do not appreciate the underlying assumptions of their codes, then the data the algorithms analyse can be compromised. According to Boyd and Crawford (2011):

> As computational scientists have started engaging in acts of social science, there is a tendency to claim their work as the business of facts and not interpretation. A model may be mathematically sound, an experiment may seem valid, but as soon as a researcher seeks to understand what it means, the process of interpretation has begun. This is not to say that all interpretations are created equal, but rather that not all numbers are neutral.

Researchers such as Williamson (2015) warn that these biases may result in a hierarchy between those that create MOOC systems and those who use these courses and systems, such that empowered 'producers' of technical systems indirectly can overly influence and exploit the student consumers of the systems. To aim for equality, we need to engage with and interpret the qualitative narratives of individual MOOC learners.

4.5 Qualitative Narratives and Learners' Stories

> Inequalities persist even for those people who do get to take part. In particular, experiences and outcomes of education differ considerably according to who someone is – what is often referred to as 'inequalities of participation'. (Selwyn 2016, p. 31).

Engaging with the qualitative narratives of individual MOOC participants enables a richer perspective of what it means to learn in a MOOC. An example of a MOOC where we have gathered narratives of how learners have learned is *Introduction to Data Science* (https://www.coursera.org/course/datasci). This MOOC was offered in 2014 by the University of Washington on the Coursera platform. The course was designed for people with a moderate level of programming experience. Over 8 weeks, 50,000 learners, from 197 countries participated in the course.

The course homepage, illustrated in Fig. 4.1, provided information about the course aims and instructional design.

To achieve the course aims, learners were expected to engage in a number programming activities, supplemented by educational materials including video lectures (Fig. 4.2).

Learner interactions were enabled through sharing data science examples (see Fig. 4.3), uploading assignments, engaging in online discussions within the MOOC platform as well as collaboration through other social media sites, including OpenStack, an online site commonly used by computer scientists to share codes and discuss coding problems. Through creating and sharing computer codes, the learners independently structured informal learning and combined this with the formal learning activities within the MOOC. This ability to personalise learning outcomes was important for professional learners who wanted to align their learning in the MOOC with their job.

Fig. 4.1 IDS MOOC Introduction Page

Below are the narrative stories of the four types of MOOC learner outlined in the typology in Chap. 3. These portraits are drawn from the stories of actual learners, who participated in the Introduction to Data Science MOOC. These narratives are part of a larger study examining the self-regulated learning of 788 participants in the MOOC (https://www.coursera.org/specializations/data-science). Quantitative data was collected through a survey posted on the course message board. Participants who completed the survey were invited to participate in an interview to explore their experiences. 32 learners were interviewed via Skype. Their narrative accounts of being a MOOC learner demonstrate the diversity of motivations, goals, learning behaviours and perspectives of the participants.

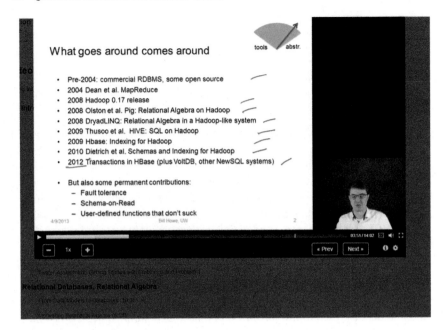

Fig. 4.2 IDS MOOC Video Lecture

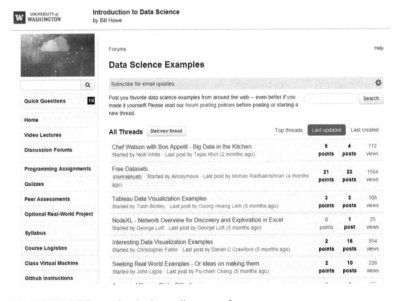

Fig. 4.3 IDS MOOC Forum for sharing coding examples

The invisible agent

It's very important for me to improve my knowledge base because I want to ensure that I am keeping up to date with the latest ideas and thinking. The MOOC is related to my profession. But I did it, not because I had to, but because I was interested in expanding my knowledge and my skill set.

I'm a fairly independent learner and feel like I am good at knowing what I need to do in order to learn the content and skills that I want to learn. I have the strength of quickly being able to tackle the problem and search for results on Internet sites, you know Google, forums and things like that. So, I think I have that strength where I can quickly just go ahead. And I did this in the MOOC. I didn't tend to go through all of the activities or watch all of the videos. I just picked and chose the content and activities that I thought were going to help me the most. I also was very happy to go and find the information elsewhere.

When I need to learn something, I will usually try to do it myself, usually with the help of Google and textbooks rather than to seek out another person or to find a formal training opportunity. I have used those kinds of 3 avenues. I rely a lot on academic literature for things of a technical nature and I also buy a lot of books. So, I buy a lot of programming books, a lot of statistical, data science and data mining book.

I guess one thing is I am optimistic, so it means I'll try a lot of things and I kind of enjoy doing new things and that makes it I guess kind of easy for me to go out on a limb and do a whole bunch of different things and see how it goes. I'm pretty decent at…basically I work reasonably well without the interaction of other people. I didn't particularly use the direction of other people during my regular university classes or regular school classes and I don't particularly need it now. So, I guess it could be considered a strength, I don't really need to depend on other people for it.

The socialiser

The MOOC is more of a personal curiosity than a real work requirement. I'm doing it for myself. Work know that I'm doing it, but it's not a recommended thing on the company, so I'm doing it out of interest.

I think that the way I wanted to approach the MOOC was just to follow what interested me, and not worry too much about trying to keep a complete overview of the area. I wanted to find appropriate tools, and tools that can be used in a timely manner. I still completed a couple of the assignments, but I wasn't that worried that I didn't keep going right to the end. To be honest the assignment is not the best benchmark to measure your learning, it is one form of measurement, but it's not a huge one because a lot of times the assignment is just a subset of what you do. Your peers are your best reflection actually.

So, if you have someone who is doing the same thing and you talk to him or her every day, then that's the best thing actually.

I would say I now very rarely watch lectures. I will look through the slides and I will read the transcripts that are provided, the subtitles, as a high-speed way to look over the material. Then, if it isn't obvious from those two, I'll go to the lecture and only then. But I've found it a much more effective way of learning for me. I had realised that the discussion aspects were among those that suited me best because, as I saw it, I could read a book and get the same content or at least I could get equivalent content, I could watch YouTube videos and the same kind of thing. The things that were really different were the motivation from doing things with a group of people and the chance to talk things out about issues. In my personal experience, being able to talk things out has been really useful to me. So that's probably the predominant way I learn in MOOCs now.

The "conventional" learner

I was aiming to get a certificate of completion and to get a passing distinction grade out of the class. I took the course very seriously from the beginning and this meant that I planned to watch all the videos and go through all the assignments. I have at least completed all the compulsory assignments.

I've taken several MOOCs and I would say that I'm at the point now where I am very familiar with the platform and how to learn on a MOOC, at least in terms of what works for me. So I can tackle courses very efficiently when I'm doing them as a student. First of all I watch lectures and after that I try to answer all the quizzes and questions, and after that I go to programme assignments.

If there is a quiz which actually makes you think it generally drives you to read more things, to discuss with your friends and generally helps you build your knowledge a lot.

I made a little Excel spreadsheet with the key dates. So, for example, I knew an assignment had to be handed in on a certain day or I knew a quiz had to be handed in on a certain day, or I knew a course project had to be handed in on a certain date. So then I guess I sort of kept track of what lectures I'd need to have covered before I could answer those questions and I kept that in mind. So I kind of planned my way through it, so I didn't miss any of the hard deadlines.

I think that the forums are very important because all the classmates could have the same problems that I have and I think the forums are very important for all the courses. When I'm working on a quiz or an assessment I like to go into the discussion forums. And it's the collaboration around the assessments that I will get involved with on the forums. This is the type of collaboration on the discussion forums that I will get involved in.

The cautious student

We've got a bit contract with the health service and that's coming to an end now, so they're trying to move all out skills into a different area, so we've been encouraged to learn a new database technology like NoSQL, analytics and so this course just fitted that learning requirement. I hadn't done any professional learning for a couple of years, although I always feel I try and learn every day if possible, but I hadn't done a course with coursework for at least 5 or 6 years.

My primary goal is not to learn, but to complete the course so I can get certified statement of accomplishment. So I definitely set out to watch all the videos and the content provided and try to solve all the assignments, although not necessarily to take part in the additional optional assignments. I am motivated by the reward of getting a certificate. But my learning strengths? I don't think I have anything particular on this one. I always think if I start something then I finish it. So I just want to keep this up.

I'm a designer so I find picking up a new thing is not that difficult, but it takes time to really be good at it, to be comfortable with it. Some of the assignments were quite a challenging task for me and I had to spend 3 days on one of the assignments. It took me quite a bit of time. Sometimes it's hard for me to gauge how much I've understood.

I watched the lectures and then I did the assignments and if I found something that I didn't know, but it was really specific to the language, let's say Python function names, then I Googled. I didn't talk to anyone. I occasionally went onto the forum to read, but I didn't ask questions on the forum. I mean it was mostly general chit chat, but if I had a problem I'd do a search on it and then it's just a matter of looking through all the responses, trying to find answers to problems.

4.6 Making Sense of the Learner Stories

One of the most impenetrable features of a MOOC is the variability in the degree to which learners engage in the course. Analysis of publically available data on MOOCs shows a positive correlation between course length and total number enrolments, but a negative correlation between course length and completion (Jordan 2014). However, as learner stories one and two above demonstrate, not completing is not synonymous with not learning.

At the same time completion, or at least engaging with all of the content and participating in learning activities, is not necessarily indicative of learning or of the learner's ability to participate in a MOOC. As learner story four (the cautious student) illustrated, this individual was less concerned with learning, and, indeed, at many stages struggled to regulate their learning behaviour and actions to maximise their experience. Instead, this learner was motivated by a need, imposed by their workplace, to undertake professional development.

The potential perils of MOOCs and online learning, and their inability to adequately support the learning of all students is identified by Selwyn (2016) who contended:

> The assumption that all individuals can navigate their own pathways through digital education opportunities implies a corresponding withdrawal of expert direction, guidance and support. While offering an alternative to the perceived paternalism of organised education provision, this approach does bump up against the widely held belief in education that learning is a social endeavour that is best supported by more knowledgeable others. (p. 73)

Selwyn highlights two themes that emerged from the learner stories narrated above. The first theme is that individuals are able to adequately regulate their learning behaviours and actions, and the second theme is the level of social engagement and interaction that occurs in a MOOC.

Stories one, two and three portrayed learners who demonstrated relatively high levels of self-regulation during their engagement in the MOOC. All three were able to shape their learning in order to reach their desired goals. The variation in their engagement during the MOOC reflected how the course was situated within the individual contexts and interests of each learner. These three learners were able to employ a range of learning behaviours and to pursue different pathways, in order to meet their different goals and outcomes. They had the skills necessary to actively and very deliberately determine the nature of their engagement, aligning their behaviours with their course goals and personal ambitions.

Some MOOC providers have recognised this need to provide variation in engagement and have designed courses to crowdsource data in areas of contemporary social interest. For example, three MOOCs from the University of Edinburgh (UK) used this strategy. A MOOC on Behavioural Economics invited learners to participate in an analysis of European dietary choices; a group of astrobiologists created an international community of people interested in research into life on other planets; and, in 2014 during the run-up to the Scottish Independence referendum, a group of political science academics ran a number of opinion polls during the MOOC 'Toward Scottish Independence? Understanding the Referendum'. These opinion and data gathering activities helped to sustain engagement throughout each MOOC. There were signs of reduced engagement, although the rate of reducing activity within these MOOCs over time was less striking than in many other MOOCs. Though it is difficult to link sustained learner engagement with the MOOC activities, or their connection with current affairs and events outside the MOOC.

Selwyn (2016) identified the absence of socialisation in much online learning. MOOCs allow opportunities for massive numbers of learners to develop through mutual forms of engagement. However, there is evidence that many MOOC learners do most of their learning on their own (see, for example Littlejohn et al. 2016; Alario-Hoyos et al. 2014). Yet learners' behaviour may be similar whether the MOOC is run as a live event (in-session, instructor-led with the opportunity to earn a certificate) or as an archived course (standalone materials, self-directed course with minimal instructional support and peer student presence, no deadlines, no peer-assessment, and no opportunity to earn credit) (Campbell et al. 2014). Even when there are many people learning at the same time, learners may choose to work on their own, rather than taking the opportunity to learn with other people. One reason may be because the course design offers few opportunities to interact with other people (Margaryan et al. 2015).

MOOC learners find ways to organise themselves, finding ways to create opportunities for interaction. In some MOOCs students plan collaboration and interaction via social media (e.g. Facebook, WhatsApp, etc.) or with colleagues, family and friends (Lin et al. 2015). Other learners organise face-to-face meet-ups in locations around the world (Lin et al. 2015; Vale and Littlejohn 2014).

Less-experienced learners may find it challenging to understand how to engage in a MOOC (Milligan et al. 2013), particularly where there is no overall course summary or well-defined structure to scaffold their learning (Kop et al. 2011). In the learner stories above, learner four struggled to determine his own learning journey and consequently used the predefined, linear course structure to scaffold his learning. In cases where MOOCs lack a clear structure or predefined learning journey, community and peer support become more important. Learners who are unable to chart their own learning pathways may rely on others to help scaffold their learning. They might follow other learners' pathways and actions, or seek advice as to their next steps. However, not all learners feel comfortable engaging socially or collaboratively in a MOOC setting (Milligan and Littlejohn 2016). Therefore, the student experience is likely to be different depending on each individual's prior learning experience.

Research has found that learner discussions and interactions on a MOOC tend to be characterised by decreasing participation over time (Jordan 2014). There is evidence that some conversations are restricted because the students have limited experience and knowledge to drive forward analysis of key concepts (Sinha et al. 2014). People sometimes post their own perceptions and anecdotal evidence, which may lead to the development of surface, rather than deep, analysis and dialogue. Generally, MOOC learners have limited opportunities for one-to-one dialogue with people who have more expertise or with tutors, particularly when the ratio of tutors to students is thousands to one. Yet it is this sort of engagement with an expert that might help to sustain interaction.

Another characteristic of discussion forums is that people with similar interests and knowledge may work together, giving rise to a phenomenon termed 'homophily'. On the one hand, learning with people of similar interests and ability can be beneficial (Wegerif 1998). On the other hand, homophily can lead to a narrowing of knowledge and ideas, which can lead to high levels of activity and engagement within a MOOC, leading to narrow knowledge development (Sinha et al. 2014).

Gillani and Eynon (2014) examined tens of thousands of comments in MOOC discussion forums across a range of MOOCs. Their findings indicated that learners may participate in discussions without completing assignments (like learner two in the narratives above). They further detected declining participation in the discussion forum over time. Over time the discussion participants formed small groups, with 20% of the participants contributing to 90% of the overall discussion. The motivations for participating in the discussion varied, depending on the course and the learner, and ranged from seeking help to contributing ideas.

These types of interactions are indicative of critical peer-supported learning processes. Where learners are not supported directly in a MOOC by tutors or experts, peer support becomes more crucial. Peer learning is supported by a number of technologies, both within the course on the MOOC platform and outside the course boundary, via learners' self-selected digital tools, such as Facebook and Twitter, and also in non-digital settings (Kellogg et al. 2014; Shen and Kuo 2015; Sinha et al. 2014).

Sentiment analysis of a student's contributions to a social media site or forum is being investigated by Rosé and colleagues to support deeper analysis of affective factors influencing learning (see, for example Yang et al. 2014). Learners may learn more effectively when they are happy or when they feel challenged, though these characteristics are likely to be tightly bound to the learner, rather than being general factors (Boekaerts 1993). There is a view that using data analytics to gather information about learners' characteristics and motivations can help to design more attractive courses and promote engagement, which may lead to better retention, engagement and learning (Rienties and Rivers 2014).

What makes these measurements difficult is that these characteristics and motivations extend beyond the boundaries of the MOOC; a learner may elect to drop out of a MOOC because of a competing priority in her life. This situation emphasises first the importance of gathering a broad range of data that enables engagement with learner stories and narratives to complement the use of data analytics, and second, that data associated with learners are dynamic and change over time—a learner may intent to complete a MOOC then change her mind.

The fourth learner story illustrated above highlights the less empowered and agentic MOOC learner. Learners who tend towards the fourth learner story typically have less experience in self-directing their own learning and in deliberately modifying their learning behaviours and actions in order to learn in the ways that are most relevant to them. This type of learner might benefit from engaging in regulatory activities, such as *planning* what they will do in the MOOC, *monitoring* and *controlling* these activities, and *self-reflecting and evaluating* their own learning (Milligan et al. 2012). However, this chapter has illustrated that, given the apparent inability to fully understand the nature of learning occurring through quantitative measures alone, and the complexity of gathering and analysing qualitative data, designing high quality, responsive learning on MOOCs is highly challenging.

MOOCs need to accommodate learners with—at certain times—opposed intentions, motivations and goals. The learners themselves come with very different learning approaches, prior experiences and confidence in managing and directing their own learning. Learners further are seeking significant variety in levels of social inter-action and engagement in a MOOC. Given this diversity, understanding what makes a 'good' or 'high quality' MOOC is an incredibly challenging question to answer. Chapter 5 attempts to unpack the complexities around notions of quality in MOOCs.

4.7 Concluding Thoughts

The diversity of learners engaging with MOOCs has been well documented. And there is a growing body of research exploring the learning implications associated with this diversity. What we have attempted to argue in this chapter is the need to ensure that this diversity is understood in a holistic, contextually mediated way. This requires a move beyond current limits of quantitative data and learning analytics. Learning is a deeply personal, context-dependent (which of course includes a social dimension) undertaking. In order to fully appreciate the diversity of learning and learners in MOOCs, it is necessary to engage with the qualitative learning stories of individual learners. While the quest to open up access to massive numbers of learners is a noble task, the reality is that deep learning will only be successful when each individual learner is supported to engage in the learning process. This centrality of the individual learner in discussions about quality in MOOCs, will be explored in greater detail in Chap. 5.

Acknowledgments The authors wish to thank Vicky Murphy of The Open University for comments and for proofing this chapter.

References

Abeer, W., & Miri, B. (2014). Students' preferences and views about learning in a MOOC. *Procedia—Social and Behavioral Sciences, 152,* 318–323.

Alario-Hoyos, C., Perez-Sanagustin, M., Cormier, D., & Delgado-Kloos, C. (2014). Proposal for a conceptual framework for educators to describe and design MOOCs. *Journal of Universal Computer Science, 20*(1), 6–23.

Balakrishnan, G., & Cooetzee, D. (2013). *Predicting student retention in Massive Open Online Courses using Markov models* (Report No. UCB/EECS-2013-109). Berkley, CA: University of California at Berkeley. Retrieved from https://www2.eecs.berkley.edu/Pubs/TechRpts/2013/EECS-2013-109.pdf.

Barron, B. (2006). Interest and self-sustained learning as catalysts of development: A learning ecology perspective. *Human Development, 49*(4), 193–224.

Biesta, G. (2009). Good education in an age of measurement: On the need to reconnect with the question of purpose in education. *Educational Assessment, Evaluation and Accountability, 21*(1), 33–46.

Boekaerts, M. (1993). Being concerned with well-being and with learning. *Educational Psychologist, 28*(2), 149–167.

Boyd, D., & Crawford, K. (2011, September 21). *Six provocations for big data*. SSRN. Paper presented at A Decade in Internet Time: Symposium on the Dynamics of the Internet and Society,

Oxford Internet Institute, Oxford, UK. Retrieved from https://papers.ssrn.com/sol3/papers.cfm? abstract_id=1926431.

Buckingham-Shum, S., & Deakin-Crick, R. (2012, April 29–May 2). Learning dispositions and transferable competencies: pedagogy, modelling and learning analytics. In *Proceedings of the 2nd International Conference on Learning Analytics and Knowledge* (pp. 92–101). New York, NY: ACM.

Campbell, J., Gibbs, A., Najafi, H., & Severinski, C. (2014). A comparison of learner intent and behaviour in live and archived MOOCs. *International Review of Research in Open and Distributed Learning, 15*(5), 234–262.

Cobb, P., & Bower, J. (1999). Cognitive and situated learning perspectives in theory and practice. *Educational Research, 28*(2), 4–15.

Colvin, K., Champaign, J., Liu, A., Zhou, Q., Fredericks, C., & Pritchard, D. (2014). Learning in an introductory physics MOOC: All cohorts learn equally, including an on-campus class. *International Review of Research in Open and Distributed Learning, 15*(4), 263–283.

de Waard, I., Abajian, S., Gallagher, M., Hogue, R., Keskin, N., Koutropoulos, A., et al. (2011). Using mLearning and MOOCs to understand chaos, emergence, and complexity in education. *International Review of Research in Open and Distance Learning, 12*(7), 94–115.

Downes, S. (2012). *Connectivism and connective knowledge: Essays on meaning and learning networks.* Ottawa, Canada: National Research Council Canada. Retrieved from https://pdfs. semanticscholar.org/4718/ee3c1930820e094552f0933cbc3b86548dbc.pdf.

Ebben, M., & Murphy, J. S. (2014). Unpacking MOOC scholarly discourse: A review of nascent MOOC scholarship. *Learning, Media and Technology, 39*(3), 328–345.

Emanuel, E. (2013). Online education: MOOCs taken by educated few. *Nature, 503,* 342.

Eraut, M. (1994). *Developing professional knowledge and competence.* London: Falmer.

ESMA. (2016, December 19). European Supervisory Authorities consult on big data. *European Securities and Markets Authority.* Retrieved from https://www.esma.europa.eu/press-news/ esma-news/european-supervisory-authorities-consult-big-data.

Fischer, G. (2014). Beyond hype and underestimation: Identifying research challenges for the future of MOOCs. *Distance Education, 35*(2), 149–158.

Gašević, D., Dawson, S., & Siemens, G. (2015). Let's not forget: Learning analytics are about learning. *TechTrends, 59*(1), 64–71.

Gasevic, D., Kovanovic, V., Joksimovic, S., & Siemens, G. (2014). Where is research on massive open online courses headed? A data analysis of the MOOC research initiative. *The International Review of Research in Open and Distributed Learning, 15*(5).

Gillani, N., & Eynon, R. (2014). Communication patterns in massively open online courses. *The Internet and Higher Education, 23,* 18–26.

Gillani, N., Yasserie, T., Eynon, R., & Hjorth, I. (2014). Structural limitations of learning in a crowd: Communication vulnerability and information diffusion in MOOCs. *Scientific Reports, 4,* 6447.

Greeno, J., Collins, A., & Resnick, L. (1996). Cognition and learning. In D. Berliner & R. Calfee (Eds.), *Handbook of educational psychology* (pp. 15–41). New York, NY: MacMillian.

Hakkarainen, K., & Paavola, S. (2007, February). *From monological and dialogical to trialogical approaches to learning.* Paper presented at the international workshop "Guided Construction of Knowledge in Classrooms", Hebrew University, Jerusalem.

Hew, K. (2014). Promoting engagement in online courses: What strategies can we learn from three highly rated MOOCS? *British Journal of Educational Technology, 47*(2), 320–342.

Hood, N., Littlejohn, A., & Milligan, C. (2015). Context counts: How learners' contexts influence learning in a MOOC. *Computers & Education, 91,* 83–91.

Illeris, K. (2007). *How we learn: Learning and non-learning in school and beyond.* London: Routledge.

Jiang, S., Williams, A. E., Warschauer, M., He, W., & O'Dowd, D. K. (2014). Influence of incentives on performance in a pre-college biology MOOC. *The International Review of Research in Open and Distributed Learning, 15*(5), 99–112.

Jordan, K. (2014). Initial trends in enrolment and completion of massive open online courses. *The International Review of Research in Open and Distributed Learning, 15*(1), 133–160.

Kellogg, S., Booth, S., & Oliver, K. (2014). A social network perspective on peer supported learning in MOOCs for educators. *The International Review of Research in Open and Distributed Learning, 15*(5), 265–289.

Koller, D., Ng, A., Do, C., & Chen, Z. (2013). Retention and intention in massive open online courses: In depth. *EduCause Review Online, 48*(3), 62–63. Retrieved from http://er.educause.edu/articles/2013/6/retention-and-intention-in-massive-open-online-courses-in-depth.

Kop, R., Fournier, H., & Mak, J. (2011). A pedagogy of abundance or a pedagogy to support human beings? Participant support on massive open online courses. *International Review of Research in Open and Distributed Learning, 12*(7), 74–93.

Lave, J., & Wenger, E. (1991). *Situated learning: Legitimate peripheral participation*. Cambridge, UK: Cambridge University Press.

Lin, Y. L., Lin, H. W., & Hung, T. T. (2015). Value hierarchy for massive open online courses. *Computers in Human Behaviour, 53,* 408–418.

Littlejohn, A., Hood, N., Milligan, C., & Mustain, P. (2016). Learning in MOOCs: Motivations and self-regulated learning in MOOCs. *The Internet and Higher Education, 29,* 40–48.

Liyanagunawardena, T., Adams, A., & Williams, S. (2013). MOOCs: A systematic study of the published literature 2008–2012. *International Review of Research in Open and Distributed Learning, 14*(3), 202–227.

Margaryan, A., Bianco, M., & Littlejohn, A. (2015). Instructional quality of massive open online courses (MOOCs). *Computers & Education, 80,* 77–83.

Milligan, C. (2012). Change 11 SRL-MOOC study initial findings. Blog Learning in the workplace Researching learning among knowledge workers.

Milligan, C., & Littlejohn, A. (2016). How health professionals regulate their learning in massive open online courses. *The Internet and Higher Education, 31,* 113–121.

Milligan, C., Littlejohn, A., & Margaryan, A. (2013). Patterns of engagement in connectivist MOOCs. *Journal of Online Learning and Teaching, 9*(2), 149–161.

Mor, Y., Ferguson, R., & Wasson, B. (2015). Learning design, teacher inquiry into student learning and learning analytics: A call for action. *British Journal of Educational Technology, 46*(2), 221–229.

Morozov, E. (2014, October 13). The planning machine. *The New Yorker*. Retrieved from www.newyorker.com/magazine/2014/10/13/planning-machine.

Muñoz-Merino, P., Ruiperez-Valiente, J., Alario-Hoyos, C., Perez-Sanagustin, M., & Delgado-Kloos, C. (2015). Precise effectiveness strategy for analyzing the effectiveness of students with educational resources and activities in MOOCs. *Computers in Human Behaviour, 47,* 108–118.

Nonaka, I., & Toyama, R. (2003). The Knowledge-creating theory revisited: Knowledge creation as a synthesizing process. *Knowledge Management Research and Practice, 1*(1), 2–10.

Pea, R. (1997). Practices of distributed intelligence and designs for education. In G. Salomon (Ed.), *Distributed cognitions: Psychological and educational considerations* (pp. 47–87). Cambridge, UK: Cambridge University Press.

Piaget, J. (1964). Part I: Cognitive development in children: Piaget development and learning. *Journal of Research in Science Teaching, 2*(3), 176–186.

Putnam, R., & Borko, H. (1997). Teacher learning: Implications of new views of cognition. In B. Biddle, T. Good, & I. Goodson (Eds.), *The International handbook of teachers and teaching* (pp. 1223–1296). Dordrecht, The Netherlands: Kluwer.

Rayyan, S., Seaton, D., Belcher, J., Pritchard, D., & Chuang, I. (2013, October). *Participation and performance in 8.02x Electricity and Magnetism: The first physics MOOC from MITx*. Paper presented at Physics Education Research Conference Proceedings, Portland, Oregon, US. Retrieved from http://arxiv.org/abs/1310.3173.

Rienties, B., & Rivers, B. A. (2014). Measuring and understanding learner emotions: Evidence and prospects. *Learning Analytics Review, 1,* 1–28.

Selwyn, N. (2010). Looking beyond learning: Notes towards the critical study of educational technology. *Journal of Computer Assisted learning, 26*(1), 65–73.

Selwyn, N. (2016). *Is technology good for education*. Cambridge, UK: Polity Books.

Sfard, A. (1998). On two metaphors for learning and the dangers of choosing just one. *Educational Researcher, 27*(2), 4–13.

Shen, C., & Kuo, C. (2015). Learning in massive open online courses: Evidence from social media mining. *Computers in Human Behavior, 51,* 568–577.

Sinha, T., Li, N., Jermann, P., & Dillenbourg, P. (2014, October 25). *Capturing "attrition intensifying" structural traits from didactic interaction sequences of MOOC learners.* Paper presented at the 2014 Conference on Empirical Methods in Natural Language Processing. Workshop on Modeling Large Scale Social Interaction in Massively Open Online Courses, Doha, Qatar (pp. 42–49). Taberg, Sweden: Taberg Media Group AB. Retrieved from https://www.aclweb.org/anthology/W/W14/W14-41.pdf.

Skrypnyk, O., de Vries, P., & Hennis, T. (2015, May 18–20). *Reconsidering retention in MOOCs: The relevance of formal assessment and pedagogy.* Paper presented at the Third European MOOCs Stakeholders Summit, Université catholique de Louvain, Mons, Belgium. Retrieved from https://s3.amazonaws.com/academia.edu.documents/37666738/Papers.pdf?AWSAccessKeyId=AKIAIWOWYYGZ2Y53UL3A&Expires=1503231269&Signature=IrKy647r03CIxal0L%2BVnXQFNlkQ%3D&response-content-disposition=inline%3B%20filename%3DDesign_intent_and_iteration_The_HumanMOO.pdf#page=166.

Tabba, Y., & Medouri, A. (2013). LASyM: A learning analytics system for MOOCs. *International Journal of Advanced Computer Science and Applications, 4*(5), 113–119.

Vale, K., & Littlejohn, A. (2014). Massive open online course: A traditional or transformative approach to learning. In A. Littlejohn & C. Pegler (Eds.), *Reusing open resources: Learning in open networks for work, life and education* (pp. 138–153). New York, NY: Routledge.

Vu, D., Pattison, P., & Robins, G. (2015). Relational event models for social learning in MOOCs. *Social Networks, 43,* 121–135.

Wang, Y., & Baker, R. (2015). Content or platform: Why do students complete MOOCs? *MERLOT, 11*(1), 17–30.

Wegerif, R. (1998). The social dimension of asynchronous learning networks. *Journal of Asynchronous Learning Networks, 2*(1), 34–49.

Williams, R., Karousou, R., & Mackness, J. (2011). Emergent learning and learning ecologies in Web 2.0. *The International Review of Research in Open and Distance Learning, 12*(3), 39–59.

Williamson, B. (2015, April 15–17). *Cognitive computing and data analytics in the classroom.* Paper presented at British Sociological Association Annual Conference 2015, Glasgow Caledonian University, Glasgow, UK. Retrieved from http://www.academia.edu/11968853/Cognitive_computing_and_data_analytics_in_the_classroom.

Yang, D., Wen, M., Kumar, A., Xing, E., & Rosé, C. (2014). Towards an integration of text and graph clustering methods as a lens for studying social interaction in MOOCs. *International Review of Research in Open and Distributed Learning, 15*(5), 214–234.

Chapter 5
Designing for Quality?

Abstract There are significant complexities in interpreting and measuring quality in MOOCs. In this chapter, we examine experts' perceptions of how to measure quality in MOOCs, using empirical data we gathered through conversations with MOOC specialists. In their experience, while data can be helpful in understanding quality, the metrics measured are shaped by underpinning assumptions and biases. In conventional education, it is assumed that the learner wants to follow a course pathway and complete a course. However, this assumption may not be valid in a MOOC. Quality data might not capture the underlying goals and intentions of MOOC learners. Therefore, it is difficult to measure whether or not a learner has achieved his or her goals. We stress the need to explore quality metrics from the learner's point of view and to encompass the variability in motivations, needs and backgrounds, which shape conceptions of quality for individuals.

5.1 Contested Purpose, Uncertain Quality

Establishing what denotes quality in MOOCs is a challenging proposition. Quality is not objective. It is a measure for a specific purpose. Purpose in education is a contested construct, which shifts depending on context and the perspective of the particular actor—governments, institutions, corporations, teachers and academics, researchers and learners. In traditional, formal education there has tended to be some degree of consensus between the actors involved as to the overarching purpose of a particular course, or programme, or educational pathway. In MOOCs, this common ground is much harder to identify and maintain.

Reflections and questions about quality are inextricably tied up in a series of complex questions, including: How do MOOCs transform education, for institutions involved in the creation and delivery of education, and for learners? What are the outcomes that should be expected or demanded from MOOCs? Are these outcomes consistent and static or should they vary by actor and context? How should the competing expectations and demands of MOOCs be balanced? And who should decide?

© The Author(s) 2018
A. Littlejohn and N. Hood, *Reconceptualising Learning in the Digital Age*,
SpringerBriefs in Open and Distance Education,
https://doi.org/10.1007/978-981-10-8893-3_5

MOOCs tend to be positioned as outside of traditional educational provision. And while undoubtedly pushing boundaries and calling into question existing paradigms and approaches in education, in reality they remain very much embedded within the existing power structures and control of the pre-eminent institutions and corporations. Selwyn (2014, p. 3) explains this power imbalance as a hierarchy that exists between 'those that "do" educational technology' and 'those who have educational technology "done" to them'. A hierarchy that encompasses, at its worst, dichotomous positions of producer and consumer; empowered and exploited.

While the early rhetoric positioning MOOCs as a panacea that would democratise access and outcomes in education has diminished, there remains an overzealous and frequently uncritical assumption that the new, and the digital must be good. As Selwyn (2016) explains 'the values and meanings that are attached to the *idea* of digital education could be seen as just as significant as any actual use of digital technology' (p. 8). That is, there is minimal rigorous, empirical evidence that technology consistently leads either to improved teaching practices and opportunities or to improved learning outcomes.

This chapter explores these claims and the problematic relationship between quality standards and educational innovation. Based on data gathered through our own research, we explore the notions of quality in MOOCs.

5.2   Notions of Quality

The importance not just of education but of quality education is enshrined as Goal four of the United Nation's Transforming Our World: The 2030 Agenda for Sustainable Development. It reads, 'ensure inclusive and equitable quality education and promote lifelong learning opportunities for all'. It goes on to explain in detail what this might mean and the generic outcomes it will translate to for all people around the world. However, while the broad outcomes are articulated, specific discussion of what a quality education might look like and the inputs and processes that are required to achieve the desired outcomes are notably absent. It is an absence that reflects the inability to arrive at an absolute threshold standard of quality or a definitive list of the specific criteria that quality education may be assessed against.

Gibbs (2010), in his report on quality in undergraduate education, utilised Biggs's (1993) 3P model of learning to explore notions and dimensions of quality. Biggs conceptualises education as a complex set of interacting ecosystems, with a particular programme or MOOC functioning as a single ecosystem. To understand how each educational ecosystem operates, it is necessary to break it into its constituent parts, and to explore the position and operation of each part both individually and in relation to the other parts that come together form the whole. Moreover, it is also necessary to understand how each educational ecosystem is positioned in relation to other ecologies.

Quality, therefore, is positioned as a context-dependent construct. That is, to understand quality of a MOOC (or any educational or learning opportunity and experience), it is necessary to situate the MOOC within the broader ecosystems in which it operates. Quality, therefore, must encompass the changing educational, economic, political, technological and social contexts (Hood and Littlejohn 2016a).

Biggs (1993) and Gibbs (2010) following him break any educational ecosystem into three parts: *presage, process* and *product* variables, which relate broadly to the input–environment–output model. Presage factors are the resources and factors that go into an educational experience or product. In traditional learning, common presage measures include funding and the allocation of funding into teaching, student to staff ratios across institutions, the quality of teaching staff and the quality of students entering an institution. Process variables refer to the processes and actions associated with presage variables, including pedagogical models, instructional design and learning materials. Product variables are the outputs or outcomes of educational processes, which traditionally have been measured by student retention, completion and certification, and grade levels.

These 3Ps apply to MOOCs. However, their particular composition and the measures that may be associated with them do not always transfer directly from more traditional forms of education and learning. In many cases, the aspects of MOOCs that led to early supporters labelling them as revolutionary and transformational represent a redefinition of presage, process and product variables.

In early 2016, the authors undertook a survey of MOOC experts—people who had experience in developing, researching and implementing MOOCs or MOOC platforms from around the world (Hood and Littlejohn 2016b). The purpose of the survey was to identify experts' perceptions of how to measure quality in MOOCs. To stimulate responses and to provoke an element of controversy or argumentation, the authors provided four different scenarios for approaching quality in MOOCs. Scenario one presented quality from the perspective of the learner, scenario two in relation to pedagogical approach, scenario three from an instruction design perspective and scenario four from an outputs perspective. The response from experts demonstrates the challenges in understanding what quality means in a MOOC and trying to construct and action a quality framework that will adequately accommodate the complexity and mutability of MOOCs.

Below are presented excerpts from the responses. The views expressed represent many of the ideas that will be explored in greater detail throughout this chapter.

In these first two quotes from MOOC experts, there is recognition of the multiple actors whose voice and perspectives may inform any consideration and judgment on quality in MOOCs.

According to the ISO (International Organization for Standardization), quality is defined as a set of products and services features that matches the client's demands. Client is considered anyone who uses the system. According to the American Society for Quality (2014) in technical usage, quality can have two meanings: 1. The characteristics of a product or service that rely on its ability to satisfy stated or implied needs. 2. A product or service free of deficiencies. The totality of features and characteristics of a product or service that relies on its ability to satisfy given needs. Besides the different approaches to the concept of quality, it is consensual that quality is a subjective term for which each person has her own definition.

Implicit in this description of quality is an understanding that quality is mutable and context-rich and that a person's perception of quality will be dependent on their particular orientation towards a product (or learning opportunity). That is, the producer of a MOOC, or the platform provider may have very different measures and understandings of quality to the learner. The variety of perceptions and desired outcomes of the different actors and agents involved in MOOCs led to another respondent arguing that:

> QA on MOOCs cannot be standarised as for some every online course is a MOOC and MOOCs are used for several different aims. As such the purpose for using a MOOC differ largely. Even with one MOOC there is no uniformal aims between actors involved (institution, the teaching staff involved and the participants). MOOCs are designed for various target groups, and even within 'one target group' the motivation and intention of MOOC participants vary a lot. Even the intention of one participant is likely to change during the MOOC (as it is non-formal learning). Consequently quality of MOOCs can only be measured against the design. I.e. the persons involved in QA of MOOCs must focus on a clear design principle at early start of the development of the MOOC with clear indicators at different actor/stakeholder level. And check if QA processes are in place to measure these indicators and to adjust the design of the MOOCs during next iterations. This kind of QA processes are for some part uniform, and in this way counteract that quality is context and cultural dependent.

Another respondent similarly argued the important role of design in understanding and assessing quality in MOOCs, this time making an explicit connection between the commercial motivations of MOOC providers and the need for high-quality design:

> How to measure quality depends on the goal of the MOOC: if the goal is to reach a new target group then outcome measures make sense. If the goal is to make (commercial) publicity for the organizing institution then the quality of the design and the materials is a better indication.

The importance of design could also be connected to the primacy of the learner as product (as opposed to the more traditional learning as product).

> We recognised that not only will each learner have a different response to the same course/learning environment, but could also have a different response from moment to moment. ... This considers the relationship between design (structure) and learner experience (agency), which gives an indication of the success of the MOOC (another question is whether success equates to quality). Considering quality in terms of learner experience is to think of quality as measure of a product. But quality could also be a measure of the process, i.e. the pedagogy or the instructional design. If the learner perception is one of a high quality learning experience, then by implication the pedagogy and instructional design are appropriate to their expectation. If the learner hasn't had a good experience, then it doesn't matter how many of the pedagogy or instructional design quality criteria boxes have been ticked.

The learner is positioned as the central outcome measure and design pivotal in the construction of the learner. The primacy of the learner in understandings of quality was the dominant perspective of participants. There is recognition, in particular, of the diversity of learners' participation in MOOCs and the varying motivations, learning dispositions and goals that they brought to a MOOC, as the three quotations below indicate.

> With such a diverse audience, it's very difficult to define quality in any way which doesn't take learners' experiences into account. Of course, this makes the measurement of MOOC quality difficult—because what's 'quality' for one learner may be wildly different to 'quality' for another learner. Platforms and course creators are still working out which proxies might be best used to measure quality in this context. As a starting point, many have used traditional outcome measures such as completion and certification. But this has likely led some providers to misjudge where they are being successful and where they need to improve, erroneously judging courses to be a success simply because their audiences are more comparable to those of formal education. This approach risks wasting the potential of MOOCs to open up education to less traditional types of learners and motivations, instead emphasising a focus on more traditional experiences translated into a MOOC environment.

> I'm not convinced we are able to achieve a stable measurement of quality when participants are so varied in their intentions, backgrounds and experiences. For me the best approach would include questions that aim to understand where participants are starting from (what are you hoping/expecting to get out of this course) and where they end up, over a reasonable period of time. It would also involve understanding what range of experiences the course has been designed to make possible for participants. And it would leave plenty of room for the unanticipated, and use inventive measures of engagement (like intensity of activity around particular aspects of the course; prevalence of knowledge exchange beyond the course) to try to expose surprising outcomes.

> I'm biased towards learner empowerment, meaning that I'd base MOOC quality on the job the learner wants the MOOC to do for them. For some it's enjoyment and curiosity. For others it's gaining a credential that enables them to further their career. For others it could be a mandatory requirement of a new position or framework. These are not mutually-exclusive. The thing we need to be careful about is Campbell's Law[1] which warns us against putting numbers against social indicators. This leads to pressure on increasing the number, no matter what it is. The trouble is that "caring doesn't scale, and scaling doesn't care". Which means that while xMOOCs have, up to now, been all about numbers, we might need a way to build communities. In other words, perhaps we need to go back to the original, more rhizomatic, and community-focused vision of MOOCs.

The final quotation included here identifies the subjective nature of quality, and the importance of questioning not just what but for whom. The questions this participant raises will be explored in the remainder of this chapter.

> The key seems to be the role in what measuring quality is for. It is not an objective measure—but a measure with a purpose—who would use it, why (consumer, producer or other)? I suspect the entirely valid perspectives above relate for whom the quality question is being asked (i.e. it is not without purpose and its purpose may focus the nature of the qualities being measured and promoted). Consumer—may well want to know the supplier is meeting certain quality thresholds (cognitive outcomes, engagement/fun, ease of use, employability/promotion or other social capital outcomes [networks, credibility, 'interestingness']) thresholds in deciding which MOOC (or MOOC platform) to choose. Producer—with MOOC platform competition the supplier and or platform owner may want to earn

---

[1]Campbell's law—The more any quantitative social indicator is used for social decision-making, the more subject it will be to corruption pressures and the more apt it will be to distort and corrupt the social processes it is intended to monitor.

recognition amongst their consumers and or 'Others' for reaching quality thresholds. They may just want to achieve business outcomes (brand impact, enquiry rates, income, disruption to/improvement of pedagogy value). This will depend (probably). This may of course itself depend on what consumers most value (in the end what they are willing to pay for the certificate—they may not care about pedagogic inventiveness if outcomes remain the same) alongside the business (or social mission) interests of the Producer and needs of the 3rd party. External 3rd Party—an employer/educational institute way wish to recognise 'success' in the MOOC as recognition of the competency/capacity of the individual (cognitive, or attitudinal). A government department may wish to be assured their HEIs are moving along the e-engagement pathway. It seems one 'true' measure of quality is unlikely without knowing the purpose. Quality for what and whom?

5.3 Quality of Platform Provider

The quality of the platform, and perhaps more importantly the structure and operation of the organisation that administers it, plays an important role in establishing the access, reach and design of the MOOCs. It is essential to situate any discussion of platform quality in relation to the main objectives and audience of the MOOC platform, for example, the MOOC platform provider Coursera is focused on professional training, while FutureLearn is centred on dialogic processes for more generic learning applications.

MOOC platforms have reoriented their models since their inception in 2011. Early offerings tended towards traditional university courses, organised into short chunks of learning (ten to twelve week blocks) with fixed start and end dates. Content delivery and design focused on videoed lecture content, weekly or biweekly assignments and a final exam. These early MOOCs tended to be open for access by anyone and free of charge.

Since then MOOCs have been providing increasingly flexible offerings. In particular, there has been a noticeable shift towards the more lucrative employment and professional learning or upskilling market. Some MOOCs are no longer open or free and are designed to provide professional development for specific employers, including government organisations (for example the UK tax department, Her Majesty's Revenue and Customs, HMRC), companies (for example Wellcome) and organisations such as the British Council (see the British Council MOOCs on FutureLearn at https://www.futurelearn.com/partners/british-council). MOOCs are responding both to learner behaviour and to commercial propositions, both of which pose questions for notions of quality.

MOOC platforms have been searching for sustainable business models. This has led to MOOC providers launching paid-for content or participation. Usually associated with some form of credentialing or accreditation at the end. Degree courses, such as the Computer Science Masters offered as a collaboration between Georgia Tech and Udacity, the iMBA created by Coursera and the University of Illinois, and Udacity's Nanodegrees, have also been developed for learners who specifically want to engage in a more formal, structured course of study. Udacity, in particular has partnered with corporations to provide employment-facing learning opportunities, such as the nanodegree in self-driving cars that use instructors from Mercedes-Benz and Nvidia, or the course on Android operating systems developed in conjunction with Google. Students pay $199–299 per month for these MOOCs. Udacity backs the quality of their offers by a premium version of its nanodegree, which for an extra $100 per month provides a money-back guarantee to graduates if they do not get a job within 6 months of completion. Coursera and edX both offer fully pay-for courses and the UK-based FutureLearn is launching a paid-for course as part of six postgraduate degrees from Deakin University.

When the focus shifts from opening access to education, and particularly prestigious institutions of higher learning, to the business models and commercialisation of this access and the learning that entails, conceptions of quality are altered. Quality is no longer focused on the learning, per se, but on how the learning can facilitate a consistent and profitable revenue stream. The business case for a MOOC becomes more important than the social good a MOOC could provide. And it has become evident that lifelong learners are no longer the primary target of MOOCs. While there are still opportunities to audit courses for free, the real money, and therefore the primary focus for MOOC providers, is in the professional development courses.

MOOC platform providers also are responding to what they are learning about student motivations and typical learner behaviours in MOOCs. In particular, they are recognising the greater need for flexibility in ways in which they structure and offer shorter courses. Among other things, this has led to shorter courses, which often are unbounded, that is with flexible start and end dates and softer deadlines for assignments. To respond to learner dropout rates, courses have been reduced from the original 10 to 12 weeks to 6 weeks or even micro MOOCs lasting hours. Similarly, content is structured to fit with learners' behaviour. For example, videos tend to be limited to a maximum of 6 minutes, as a majority of learners will not watch beyond this. Research has further found that including in-video quizzes or instructor slides (Guo et al. 2014; Mamgain et al. 2014) and the inclusion of subtitles and the ability to vary the video speed (Mamgain et al. 2014) have been found to increase learners' perceptions of video content.

On the surface, this responsiveness to learner behaviour and implied, if not articulated demands, is a positive step. However, it has potential unintended consequences. Decisions regarding instructional design and pedagogy are not necessarily underpinned by what is known about how people learn, or how to structure learning to support the learning process. For instance, the flexibility of course start and end dates, while allowing for greater accessibility for learners, has also led to decreasing activity on discussion forum and less peer-to-peer interaction. Flexibility impacts learner success due to a number of factors. First, the link between learners' participation in discussion forums and completion (Gillani and Eynon 2014; Kizilcec et al. 2013; Sinha et al. 2014). Second, the role that peer interactions play in supporting learning and knowledge building activities (Amo 2013; Conole 2013; Hew 2014; Margaryan et al. 2015). Third, the oppotunites for help-seeking and peer assistance that flexibility in course start and end dates facilitate (Amo 2013; Guardia et al. 2013; Hew 2014).

MOOCs also are tending to be divided into smaller chunks, focusing on more discrete areas of content or specific skills. As Shah (2016) identifies, some older courses have been split into credentials. For example, the MOOC on Probabilistic Graphical Models (developed by Coursera's co-founder Daphne Koller) has now been split into three courses and is a Coursera Specialisation in its own right. These specialisations are course designs that link several smaller MOOCs to form a larger, coherent programme of learning, although it is possible to enrol only in a single course and not undertake the whole specialisation. This breaking up of content can be linked to a quest for greater revenue and the need for MOOC platforms to make money, as discussed in general in Chap. 1. It also highlights another trend in education which is the fragmentation of content and curricula. The construction of MOOCs, and their push towards providing employment-focused skills and courses might potentially exacerbate what Cleveland (1985) describes as:

> It is a well-known scandal that our whole educational system is geared more to categorizing and analyzing patches of knowledge than to threading them together. (p. 20)

5.4   Quality of Instructor

The role of the instructor in a MOOC has important implications for the learning that occurs. However, the roles adopted by the instructor and the impact that they have vary substantially between MOOCs. To date, the three most common types of instructors in MOOCs are: (1) the distant rock star or academic celebrity lecturer; (2) the co-participant or facilitator within a network and (3) the automated processes that act as a proxy to human tutor or assessor (Bayne and Ross 2014; Rodriguez 2012). A further role has emerged recently, that of the pay-for personal mentor, who provides 1:1 feedback, email and forum support and live weekly office hours (Morrison 2014). Radically new ways to connect with instructors are emerging. Learners connect to a central hub using a mobile app which then connects them with a tutor or other forms of help (e.g. experts or peers) from around the world. A tracking system enables fees to be charged and transferred from the student to the tutor or organisation. Online assessments verify the competence and skills of the learner and their identity and a blockchain system records each transaction, so that the student has a verified set of qualification associated with him or her (Sharples and Domingue 2016).

Similar to traditional, offline courses, the instructor in a MOOC determines or mediates the pedagogical approaches that are employed, the level of teaching skill and familiarity with content, and the opportunities for instructor–learner interaction and engagement during the course period. Designing and running a MOOC is a labour-intensive activity. Kolowich (2013) determined that a MOOC typically takes over 100 h of precourse set-up time and then an additional 10 h per week during the running of the course. However, many educators are not recognised for the work they put into designing and running a MOOC, in the way their 'traditional' duties are credited. Ross et al. (2014) argue for the importance of acknowledging the complexity of teacher positions and experiences in MOOCs and how these influence learner engagement. Data suggest that the instructor has a significant impact on learner retention in MOOCs (Adamopoulos 2013). Further research suggests that instructors' participation in discussion forum activity and actively supporting learners during the running of a MOOC positively influences learning outcomes (Coetzee et al. 2015; Deslauriers et al. 2011).

5.5 Quality of Learning Design

Illeris (2007) suggests that the learner's abilities, insight and understanding are developed through the content dimension of the learning experience. That is, what the learner can do, knows and understands. Examination of content in MOOCs (or arguably any learning experience) cannot be separated from the instructional design and pedagogical frameworks within which it is situated. There is an inherent tension in MOOCs between the product and process elements of their design.

The flexibility of participation and the self-directed nature of engagement, which enable learners to self-select the learning opportunities and pathways they follow when participating in a MOOC (DeBoer et al. 2014), necessitate the re-operationalisation of many of the process variables typically involved in education. The potential massive number of learners and the diversity of participants has significant implications for the learning systems and pedagogical approaches required to support these learners. Downes (2013) suggests that this involves the consideration of how to circulate content effectively and to support meaningful interactions between learners. Tyler (1939) contends that content delivery cannot exist in isolation; the value of content is related only to the use and interpretation of the content in specific contexts. Tyler's view highlights the challenge involved in MOOC design, given the multiple, diverse contexts of individual learners.

Questions emerge regarding the balance between structure (intended to provide direction) and self-regulation, between breadth and depth of content, and whether to emphasise instruction or self-directed learning. Further questions exist around the employment of broadcast or dialogue models of delivery, whether MOOCs should offer edutainment or deep learning opportunities, and whether and how to promote homophily or diversity in learners' engagement and participation.

Research has explored how the nature and presentation of content in MOOCs influences learners' perceptions of the learning experience. Perceived richness of the course content has been found to be correlated positively with learners' perceptions of their knowledge comprehension and the quality of the learning exchanges that occur (Lin et al. 2015), as well as successful completion of a course (Adamopoulous 2013). The use and creation of high-quality, authentic resources and content (Amo 2013; Conole 2013; Margaryan et al. 2015), which are connected to practical, real-life examples (Grunewald et al. 2013; Littlejohn et al. 2016) and the opportunities for quality knowledge creation throughout the course of the MOOC (Guardia et al. 2013) are also associated with effective instructional design.

While content quality is central to learners' perceptions of the MOOC experience, Dillenbourg et al. (2014) warn that there is a danger in MOOCs to focus too heavily on the engagement of learners and the professionalism of the preparation and execution of content at the expense of learning effectiveness and the fulfilment of learning objectives. Here the concept of MOOC and learning as edutainment, and the learner as consumer, are in potential conflict with the integrity and richness of the learning experience.

Content without a corresponding focus on instructional design and pedagogical framing impacts the acquisition process, see Chap. 4 for a discussion of the acquisition in the learning process. Instructional design in MOOCs is complicated by the need to adequately accommodate the diversity of the learner population and the need to provide learning activities that cater to and support different learning styles and needs (Alario-Hoyos et al. 2014; Guardia et al. 2013; Hew 2014; Margaryan et al. 2015), while also adhering to a coherent overarching design, which incorporates support structures to scaffold the learning journey. Research suggests that effective instructional design (both in MOOCs and more broadly in any learning experience) should empower learners (Amo 2013; Guardia et al. 2013), offering opportunities for personalised learning (Istrate and Kestens 2015) which drawing on learners' individual contexts and previous experiences (Scagnoli 2012). Integral to this is a consistent vision, which provides a clear and coherent framework in which to embed the content and pedagogical approaches (Conole 2013; Istrate and Kestens 2015; Warburton and Mor 2015). The consistent vision must also facilitate a degree of autonomy and the presence of differentiated pathways and flexibility has been connected to learners' perseverance in a MOOC (Jordan 2015; Perna et al. 2014).

Appropriate use of digital technology tools is important to the design and delivery of high-quality learning experiences and opportunities (Amo 2013; Conole 2013; Guardia et al. 2013; Istrate and Kesten 2015). There is considerable opportunity to utilise learning analytics to better personalise and tailor MOOCs to learners (Daradoumis et al. 2013; Kanwar 2013; Lackner et al. 2015; Sinha et al. 2014; Tabba and Medouri 2013). Chandrasekaran et al. (2015) have called for automated methods to aid instructors in responding to student feedback and questions, while Kay et al. (2013) suggested that learning analytics can be used to better understand knowledge creation and learning processes in MOOCs. However, as outlined in Chap. 4, the application of data analytics to MOOC learning processes is complex yet often oversimplified.

5.6 Quality of Adaptability to Context

Learners and learning in MOOCs are situated within multiple contexts, spanning both online and offline dimensions. To fully understand the role and positions of these contexts, it is necessary to consider not only how the human actors or learners engage with and through them, but also how the role of nonhuman materials and entities enter, engage in and shape the spaces. The social shaping of technology and physical objects through language, practice and interactions (sometimes called socio-materiality) provide useful lenses for examining the interdependencies of MOOCs and their contexts. Kling and Courtright (2003, p. 223) position online sites from a sociotechnical perspective as being:

> … structured sociotechnically, co-configured not only by the constraints and affordances of the technologies involved but also—and primarily—by social, economic, and institutional factors.

This is similar to Fenwick's (2015) socio-materiality perspective, in which she suggests that:

> What socio-material approaches offer to educational research are resources to systematically consider both the patterns as well as the unpredictability that makes educational activity possible. They promote methods by which to recognise and trace the multifarious struggles, negotiations and accommodations whose effects constitute the 'things' in education: students, teachers, learning activities and spaces, knowledge representations such as texts, pedagogy, curriculum content, and so forth. (p. 84)

These perspectives provide a useful means for engaging with the intricate relationships that emerge between learners, technology, content and environments, with each actor actively shaping and influencing the patterns of behaviour and structuring the learning that arises.

The socialisation between individuals and groups of individuals and how this socialisation process shapes and is shaped by the technological infrastructure is a much-discussed element of learning in MOOCs. This active interweaving of different actors and materials is described by Fenwick (2015):

> Everything is *performed* into existence in webs of relations. Materials are enacted, not inert; they are matter and they matter. They *act*, together with other types of things and forces, to exclude, invite, and regulate activity. This is not arguing that objects have agency: an essay does not write itself. But its particular production is an agentic assemblage of assignment protocols and literary traditions, books and other content sources (entailing all the materialities of library lineups, slow internet browsers, fortuitous tweets etc.), post-it notes and piles of paper and iPads, the particular affordances and directives of word processing software—all working in and through human bodies and consciousness. (p. 87)

Consequently, any discussion of quality in MOOCs must consider the connections and interdependencies that are facilitated by the technological infrastructure to enable each individual learner to construct their network of learning tools and resources to support them in achieving their goals. For some learners, the network of tools and resources provided on the MOOC become their primary network of learning materials. However, interview data from participants of a 'Introduction to Data Science' MOOC offered by the University of Washington through Coursera indicate the broad range of materials they engage with.

One participant explained how he worked through a difficult assessment task, describing the rich interactions with people and resources that constitute his learning:

> I tried for a whole day, not exactly a whole day, let's say a couple of hours, but I mean I was in the office before that. I had my good friend here, my previous colleague, so we used to study together anyway, so I generally end up discussing with him first … I actually try to

solve the problems mostly myself or I generally have a close group of friends we generally discuss things and that is how I have been learning so far … so I end up getting resources from there if I need something.

Another participant described a different approach. Rather than interacting with people, he preferred to draw upon his network of learning of resources:

When I need to learn something I will usually try to do it myself, usually with the help of Google and textbooks rather than to seek out another person, other human being or to seek out a formal training opportunity. Yeah so it comes down to my imposter syndrome, I don't like admitting that I don't know things … if I run into a problem, usually in debugging something, my first port of call is to Google, you know dictionaries in Python say or something like that and that will usually throw up some stack overflow answers or some various random blog posts or the Python documentation or W3 schools or all of the stuff.

These quotes illustrate the diverse ways MOOC participants learn. It is clear that it is difficult to define a set of behaviours that can be modelled or used accurately to predict the outcomes of learning relative to the learner's goals.

However, technology and learning analytic systems have the potential to play a considerable role in iteratively shaping the learning experience on MOOCs by offering insight into learner and instructor behaviour and activity. For example, new technologies and techniques are being developed that facilitate the automated analysis of discussion in MOOCs. These include technology for analysing discussions for learning (Howley et al. 2013), the formation of discussion groups (Yang et al. 2014) and indicators of motivation, cognitive engagement and attitudes towards the course (Wen et al. 2014a, b).

5.7 Quality of Outcome

In traditional models of higher education, the most common measure used to indicate the quality of the product is the proportion of students gaining a degree, and the level at which the degree is gained (Gibbs 2010). The extents to which graduating students gain employment in a field relevant to their degree and their starting salary level are other common dimensions of quality (Gibbs 2010). The MOOC literature frequently has employed retention, completion and certification rates as measures of quality. However, given the range of motivations and goals that learners bring to their participation in MOOCs, the product in a MOOC is not standardised across all learners.

Grover et al. (2013, p. 1) suggest the question 'What makes a good MOOC?' needs to be reframed as 'How can we make a MOOC work for as many of its diverse participants as possible?'. Some educationalists have suggested a solution is to ensure the MOOC design is optimised for the maximum number of students. However, rather than emancipating the MOOC learner and enabling his or her to follow a personalised pathway, this stance forces learner to comply with an 'optimal' design.

Enabling MOOCs to work for as many diverse learners as possible requires adapting the course for the learner, not the learner for the course. This involves reconceptualising participation and achievement according to the diverse motivations, goal orientations and actions of participants (DeBoer et al. 2014). This, however, would not be easy to measure. As Biesta (2007) argues, we have a history in education of only measuring what can be easily measured, rather than that which cannot be readily measured but nonetheless may be of great importance. Biesta further explains that end up valuing whatever we can measure, whether or not it is of value to us. Morozov (2014) explains that in MOOCs, learning analytics tend to be concerned with predictive and anticipatory action, with little consideration for questions of causation or the context of consequences.

The new context of learning in MOOCs requires new measures of success and quality to capture the diversity in participant behaviours and intentions (Bayne and Ross 2014). This is a complex undertaking. It entails developing a 'nuanced, strategic, dynamic and contextual' understanding of individual learners and individual MOOCs (Mak et al. 2010, p. 280). It also fundamentally requires the reconceptualisation of what MOOCs can bring to education.

5.8   Concluding Thoughts

This chapter has identified the need to develop new measures of quality in MOOCs that take into consideration the diverse patterns of participation, which are influenced by the individual motivations and goals of learners as well as their contexts, and the subsequent range of outcomes in MOOCs. There is a need to focus quality measures more strongly around individual learners and to recognise the differentiated product variables that MOOCs enable. This push towards interpreting quality outcome measures in relation to individualised learning and individual learner outcomes represents a significant break from traditional measures of product variables. When discussing and assessing quality in MOOCs, it is necessary to situate the MOOC, the learning opportunities it provides and individual learners within the multiple ecosystems in which they interact. This new focus on the learner requires new thought and the construction of reliable measures of confidence, experience and motivation, which extend beyond self-report, could provide a more accurate view of quality than conventional learner metrics.

Acknowledgements The authors wish to thank Vasudha Chaudhari of The Open University for comments and for proofing this chapter.

References

Adamopoulos, A. (2013). What makes a great MOOC? An interdisciplinary analysis of student retention in online courses. Paper presented at the Thirty-Fourth International Conference on Information Systems, Milan, Italy. Retrieved from http://pages.stern.nyu.edu/~padamopo/What%20makes%20a%20great%20MOOC.pdf.

Alario-Hoyos, C., Perez-Sanagustin, M., Cormier, D., & Delgado-Kloos, C. (2014). Proposal for a conceptual framework for educators to describe and design MOOCs. *Journal of Universal Computer Science, 20*(1), 6–23.

Amo, D. (2013, November). MOOCs: Experimental approaches for quality in pedagogical and design fundamentals. Paper presented at TEEM'13, Salamanca, Spain.

Bayne, S., & Ross, J. (2014). MOOC pedagogy. In P. Kim (Ed.), *Massive open online courses: The MOOC revolution* (pp. 23–45). New York, NY: Routledge.

Biesta, G. (2007). Why "what works" won't work: Evidence-based practice and the demcrative deficit in educational research. *Educational Theory, 57*(1), 1–22.

Biggs, J. (1993). From theory to practice: A cognitive systems approach. *Higher Education Research & Development, 12*(1), 73–85.

Chandrasekaran, M., Ragupathi, K., Kan, M., & Tan, B. (2015, December). Towards feasible instructor intervention in MOOC discussion forums. Paper presented at the Thirty-Sixth International Conference on Information Systems, Fort Worth, TX.

Coetzee, D., Lim, S., Fox, A., Hartmann, B., & Hearst, M. A. (2015). Structuring interactions for large-scale synchronous peer learning. In *Proceedings of the 18th ACM Conference on Computer- Supported Cooperative Work and Social Computing (CSCW)*, Vancouver, Canada (pp. 1139–1152). New York, NY: ACM.

Conole, G. (2013). MOOCs as disruptive technologies: Strategies for enhancing the learner experience and quality of MOOCs. *RED—Revista de Educación a Distancia, 39*. Retrieved from http://www.um.es/ead/red/39/conole.pdf.

Daradoumis, T., Bassi, R., Xhafa, F., & Caballé, S. (2013, October). A review on massive e-learning (MOOC) design, delivery and assessment. In *2013 Eighth International Conference on P2P, Parallel, Grid, Cloud and Internet Computing (3PGCIC)* (pp. 208–213). Piscataway, NJ: IEEE.

DeBoer, J., Ho, A., Stump, G. S., & Breslow, L. (2014). Changing "course": Reconceptualizing educational variables for massive open online courses. *Educational Researcher, 43*(2), 74–84. https://doi.org/10.3102/0013189X14523038.

Deslauriers, L., Schelew, E., & Wieman, C. (2011). Improved learning in a large-enrolment physics class. *Science, 332*(6031), 862–864.

Dillenbourg, P., Fox, A., Kirchner, C., Mitchell, J., & Wirsing, M. (2014). Massive open online courses: Current state and perspectives. *Manifesto from Dagstuhl Perspectives Workshop*. https://doi.org/10.4230/DagMan.4.1.1.

Downes, S. (2013, April 24). The quality of massive open online courses. Retrieved from http://mooc.efquel.org/files/2013/05/week2-The-quality-of-massive-open-online-courses-StephenDownes.pdf.

Fenwick, T. (2015). Sociomateriality and learning: A critical approach. In D. Scott & E. Hargreaves (Eds.), *The SAGE handbook of learning (online)*. London: SAGE.

Gibbs, G. (2010). *Dimensions of quality*. York, UK: The Higher Education Academy.

Gillani, N., & Eynon, R. (2014). Communication patterns in massively open online courses. *Internet and Higher Education, 23*, 18–26.

Grover, S., Franz, P., Schneider, E., & Pea, R. (2013). The MOOC as distributed intelligence: Dimension of a framework an evaluation of MOOCs. Paper presented at the 10th Annual International Conference on Computer Supported Collaborative Learning, Madison, WI. Retrieved from http://life-slc.org/docs/LSLC_rp_A194_Grover-etal_CSCL2013_MOOCsand-DI_Volume%202_CSCL2013.pdf.

Grunewald, F., Meinel, C., Totschnig, M., & Willems, C. (2013). Designing MOOCs for the support of multiple learning styles. In *Conference Proceedings from EC-TEL 2013*, LNCS (pp. 371–382). Berlin, Germany: Springer.

Guardia, L., Maina, M., & Sangra, A. (2013). MOOC design principles: A pedagogical approach from the learner's perspective. *eLearning Papers, 33*, 1–5.

Guo, P., Kim, J., & Rubin, R. (2014). How video production affects student engagement: An empirical study of MOOC videos. In *Proceedings of the First ACM conference on Learning @ Scale Conference* (pp. 41–50). New York, NY: ACM.

Hew, K. (2014). Promoting engagement in online courses: What strategies can we learn from three highly rated MOOCS? *British Journal of Educational Technology, 47*(2), 320–342. https://doi.org/10.1111/bjet.12235.

Hood, N., & Littlejohn, A. (2016a). MOOC Quality: A call for new quality measures. *Journal of Learning for Development, 3*(3), 28–42 https://t.co/EePAUPWnDb.

Hood, N., & Littlejohn, A. (2016b). *Quality in MOOCs, surveying the terrain* (Commonwealth for Learning Report). http://oasis.col.org/handle/11599/2352.

Howley, I., Mayfield, E., & Rosé, C. P. (2013). Linguistic analysis methods for studying small groups. In C. Hmelo-Silver, A. O'Donnell, C. Chan, & C. Chin (Eds.), *The international handbook of collaborative learning* (pp. 184–202). New York, NY: Routledge.

Illeris, K. (2007). *How we learn: Learning and non-learning in school and beyond*. London: Routledge.

Istrate, O., & Kestens, A. (2015, April). Developing and monitoring a MOOC: The IFRC experience. Paper presented at the 11th International Scientific Conference eLearning and Software for Education, Bucharest, Romania. Retrieved from http://www.academia.edu/14707457/DEVELOPING_AND_MONITORING_A_MOOC_THE_IFRC_EXPERIENCE.

Jordan, K. (2015). Massive open online course completion rates revisited: Assessment, length and attrition. *International Review of Research in Open and Distributed Learning, 16*(3), 341–358.

Kanwar, A. (2013, October 16). Quality vs. quantity: Can technology help? Opening keynote presentation at the 25th ICDE World Conference, Tianjin, China.

Kay, J., Reimann, P., Diebold, E., & Kummerfeld, B. (2013). MOOCs: So many learners, so much potential …. *IEEE Intelligent Systems, 28*(3), 70–77 (Kizilcic et al., 2013).

Kizilcec, R., Piech, C., & Schneider, E. (2013). Deconstructing disengagement: Analyzing learner subpopulations in massive open online courses. *LAK'13* Leuven, Belgium.

Kling, R., & Courtright, C. (2003). Group behavior and learning in electronic forums: A sociotechnical approach. *The Information Society, 19*, 221–235.

Kolowich, S. (2013, March 18). The professors behind the MOOC hype. *The Chronicle of Higher Education*. Retrieved from http://chronicle.com/article/The-Professors-Behind-the-MOOC/137905/.

Lackner, E., Ebner, M., & Khalil, M. (2015). MOOCs as granular systems: Design patterns to foster participant activity. *eLearning Papers, 42*, 28–37.

Lin, Y.-L., Lin, H.-W., & Hung, T.-T. (2015). Value hierarchy for massive open online courses. *Computers in Human Behaviour, 53*, 408–418.

Littlejohn, A., Hood, N., Milligan, C., & Mustain, P. (2016). Learning in MOOCs: Motivations and self-regulated learning in MOOCs. *The Internet and Higher Education, 29*, 40–48. https://doi.org/10.1016/j.iheduc.2015.12.003.

Mak, S., Williams, R., & Mackness, J. (2010). Blogs and forums as communication and learning tools in a MOOC. In L. Dirckinck-Holmfeld, V. Hodgson, C. Jones, M. de Laat, D. McConnell, & T. Ryberg (Eds.), In *Proceedings of the 7th International Conference on Networked Learning 2010* (pp. 275–284). Lancaster, UK: Lancaster University. Retrieved from https:// www.lancaster.ac.uk/fss/organisations/netlc/past/nlc2010/abstracts/PDFs/Mak.pdf.

Mamgain, N., Sharma, A., & Goyal, P. (2014). Learner's perspective on video-viewing features offered by MOOC providers: Coursera and edX. Paper presented at the 2014 IEEE International Conference on MOOC, Innovation and Technology in Education (MITE). https://doi.org/10.1109/mite.2014.7020298.

Margaryan, A., Bianco, M., & Littlejohn, A. (2015). Instructional quality of massive open online courses (MOOCs). *Computers & Education, 80*, 77–83.

Morozov, E. (2014). The planning machine. *The New Yorker*, 13 October (www.newyorker.com/magazine/2014/10/13/planning-machine.

Morrison, D. (2014, January 18). Need-to-know-news: MOOC mentors for hire, Coursera's MOC$s, edX shares MOOC data and more. *Online Learning Insights*. Retrieved from https://onlinelearninginsights.wordpress.com/2014/01/28/need-to-know-news-mooc-mentors-forhire-courseras-mocs-edx-shares-mooc-data-and-more/.

Perna, L., Ruby, A., Boruch, R., Wang, N., Scull, J., Ahmad, S., et al. (2014). Moving through MOOCs: Understanding the progression of users in massive open online courses. *Education Researcher, 43*(9), 421–432.

Rodriguez, C. (2012). MOOCs and the AI-Stanford like courses: Two successful and distinct course formats for massive open online courses. *European Journal of Open, Distance and E-Learning*. Retrieved from http://files.eric.ed.gov/fulltext/EJ982976.pdf.

Ross, J., Sinclair, C., Knox, J., & Macleod, H. (2014). Teacher experiences and academic identity: The missing components of MOOC pedagogy. *Journal of Online Learning and Teaching, 10*(1), 57.

Scagnoli, N. (2012). Thoughts on instructional design for MOOCs. Retrieved from https://www.ideals.illinois.edu/bitstream/handle/2142/44835/Instructional%20Design%20of%20a%20MOOC.pdf.

Selwyn, N. (2014). *Distrusting educational technology*. London and New York: Routledge.

Selwyn, N. (2016). *Is technology good for education*. Cambridge, UK: Polity Books.

Shah, D. (2016). By the numbers: MOOCS in 2016. [Online]. Retrieved from: https://www.class-central.com/report/mooc-stats-2016/.

Sharples, M., & Domingue, J. (2016, September). The blockchain and kudos: A distributed system for educational record, reputation and reward. In *European Conference on Technology Enhanced Learning* (pp. 490–496). Springer International Publishing.

Sinha, T., Li, N., Jermann, P., & Dillenbourg, P. (2014). Capturing "attrition intensifying" structural traits from didactic interaction sequences of MOOC learners. In *Proceedings of the 2014 Conference on Empirical Methods in Natural Language Processing. Workshop on Modeling Large Scale Social Interaction in Massively Open Online Courses* (pp. 42–49). Retrieved from https://www.aclweb.org/anthology/W/W14/W14-41.pdf.

Tabba, Y., & Medouri, A. (2013). LASyM: A learning analytics system for MOOCs. *International Journal of Advanced Computer Science and Applications, 4*(5), 113–119.

Tyler, K. (1939). Recent developments in radio education. *The English Journal, 28*(3), 193–199.

Warburton, S., & Mor, Y. (2015). Double loop design: Configuring narratives, patterns and scenarios in the design of technology enhanced learning. In M. Maina et al. (Eds.), *The art and science of learning design* (pp. 93–104). Rotterdam, The Netherlands: Sense Publishers.

Wen, M., Yang, D., & Rosé, C. P. (2014a). Linguistic reflections of student engagement in massive open online courses. In *Proceedings of the International Conference on Weblogs and Social Media*. Retrieved from http://www.cs.cmu.edu/~mwen/papers/icwsm2014-camera-ready.pdf.

Wen, M., Yang, D., & Rosé, C. P. (2014b). Sentiment analysis in MOOC discussion forums: What does it tell us? In *Proceedings of Educational Data Mining*. Retrieved from http://www.cs.cmu.edu/~mwen/papers/edm2014-camera-ready.pdf.

Yang, D., Wen, M., Kumar, A., Xing, E., & Rosé, C. (2014). Towards an integration of text and graph clustering methods as a lens for studying social interaction in MOOCs. *International Review of Research in Open and Distributed Learning, 15*(5). Retrieved from http://www.irrodl.org/index.php/irrodl/article/view/1853/3083.

Chapter 6
A Crisis of Identity? Contradictions and New Opportunities

Abstract Drawing on the previous chapters, this chapter explores four tensions that characterise MOOCs. Although MOOCs are seen as an attempt to democratise education, they often privilege the elite, rather than acting as an equaliser. MOOCS are also considered a way to radically open access to education, yet they tend to offer education to people who are already able to learn rather than providing opportunities for everyone. While MOOCs are positioned as a disrupting force, often they replicate the customs and values associated with formal education, rather than unsettling educational norms. MOOCs are conceived as social networks that allow learners to learn through dialogue with others, yet many learners have limited interactions with others. Even when learners have the ability to learn autonomously, they often are expected to conform to course rules, rather than deciding their own learning strategies. These problems may be accentuated where MOOCs are viewed as a set of products (content and credentials) on sale to student consumers, rather than as a transformational educational experience for learners. The view of MOOCs as a product for the consumer learner may overly simplify the complex, transformational processes that underscore learning. Particularly where underlying automated systems try to improve progression by quantifying learners' behaviours and 'correcting' these to fit an 'ideal' learner profile or where algorithms and metrics are based on convectional education, rather than on future-facing forms of learning. This chapter examines these problems with MOOCs, offering promising future directions.

6.1 When Actions Contradict Aims

This book has exposed a number of inconsistencies that characterise MOOCs. These courses are viewed by educationalists as a form of democratisation and in Chap. 2 we examined whether and how MOOCs democratise the education landscape. Democracy is a levelling force that encourages equality. So it seems puzzling that, by foregrounding the norms and power structures of pre-eminent institutions and corporations, MOOCs might emphasise, rather than diminish, inequality. MOOCs are also considered a disruptive force, with the potential to challenge existing education models. Paradoxically, MOOCs sometimes reinforce conventions by requiring

© The Author(s) 2018
A. Littlejohn and N. Hood, *Reconceptualising Learning in the Digital Age*,
SpringerBriefs in Open and Distance Education,
https://doi.org/10.1007/978-981-10-8893-3_6

learners to conform to accepted 'ways of being', a phenomenon which was explored in Chap. 3. In Chap. 4, we interrogated how MOOCs accommodate massive numbers of learners and discovered that many learners learn on their own. We concluded that, rather than opening up education to everyone, MOOCs tend to create opportunities for people who are already able to learn. Chapter 5 signalled a need to rethink the metrics and measures that signal success. Retaining conventional metrics and measures may inadvertently create a new order between those who have control of course designs and data and learners, particularly where course designs are linked to data and analytics-based decisions. More worryingly, learners may be being exploited to achieve the economic and performance outcomes preferred by the providers of MOOCs, rather than being supported to achieve their own ideal outcomes.

These inconsistencies are apparent in other forms of open, online education, not only MOOCs, so the issues highlighted in this book likely affect many different areas of online education and lifelong learning. In this chapter, we further examine these issues, in relation to their broader social, political and economic contexts, to identify ways forward both for MOOCs and online education more generally. We focus specifically on the promise of MOOCs as a democratising force and as a means to disrupt and reorientate education. The success of MOOCs and future open, online learning is linked to the ability of learners to learn. Thus, we emphasise the importance of focusing attention on preparing learners to learn in a freeform manner in open and unstructured environments, over designing courses to support masses of learners to follow course pathways.

6.2 Restraining Elitism, Embracing Democracy

An asset of MOOCs that is underutilised is their unbounded geographical locations. Moving away from the idea of a geographically located institution that offers courses in a single, physical location means that learners and academics no longer have to be scholars in a single institution, allowing them to work across numerous academies and sites. These changes could disrupt the system of networking and cronyism that originated in social class systems and has pervaded the elite universities for centuries, maximising return for the members of these institutions. And indeed there have been examples of MOOCs breaking open the stronghold of elite institutions, either by identifying exceptional students who otherwise would not have applied to attend the universities or by offering for-credit courses or degree programmes. However, these continue to be the exception rather than the rule.

More commonly, rather than using MOOCs as a way to equalise, they are viewed as a way to offer organisations a global perspective. In the previous chapters, we illustrated how MOOCs can be used as networks of communication and control to strengthen and solidify the dominance of pre-eminent universities over larger and wider groups of people globally. MOOC platforms, with their non-geospatial location, allow universities and organisations to rescale their authority from the level of the institution to the level of 'the global'. MOOCs are being used in ways that support universities to build transnational identities that affords greater global reach, reinforcing their worldwide dominance. In this way, MOOCs amplify divisions between elite institutions and organisations other education providers, rather than filling the gaps. This expansion of 'global brands' feeds the corporate interests of the organisations that provide MOOCs—universities, industry and MOOC platform providers. However, there are ways to restrain elitism and provide democratic solutions.

There is a drive from Governments and Non-Governmental Organisations (NGOs) worldwide to focus on inclusion agendas, with a commitment to 'make all voices count' and 'leave no one behind'. This agenda is important for civil society effectiveness, particularly for building capacity in countries where diversity is increasing. While diversity is increasing in the US, Canada, Australia, New Zealand and the European Union, there is also migration to and within Africa, parts of Asia and South America. So, there is a need for globally responsive, democratic education spaces that bring people together in informal and relatively unstructured networks to engage critically with concepts, and work collectively to generate new knowledge.

Democratic spaces are important for groups of learners who are under-represented or undervalued by society. For example, migrants reorienting themselves in a new place of residence, minority groups seeking to advance their views or specialist communities who want to exchange and share their knowledge. The work of NGOs in supporting learning for these groups offers a blueprint for ways in which MOOCs could become democratic.

One example is Kiron, a non-governmental organisation based in Germany that works with refugees to help them learn how to live and work in the country. Kiron uses MOOCs as a platform from which to allow refugees to begin their study in their new country of residence, as illustrated in the case example.

Case Example: Supporting refugees' learning

Refugees need support in facing the challenges of fleeing from their home countries and starting over elsewhere. Yet, they have limited opportunities to begin or continue their studies or even to learn about the new culture and context where they are living. Kiron is an NGO that works with partner universities to offer MOOCs to refugees in camps in Germany (www.kiron.ngo). They use a combination of MOOC courses, online collaboration platforms and in-person learner support to help refugee learners. Each learner selects a cluster of MOOCs bundled into modules that form coherent educational programmes. Kiron negotiates recognition of prior learning with the partner universities, who can award up to 60 credits for completed Kiron modules using the European Credit Transfer and Accumulation System (ECTS). The MOOC-based study means that refugees can continue to learn even if they have to move geographically. After 2 years, Kiron students can apply to a partner university to complete the third and fourth year of study for a Bachelor's degree.

The case example from Kiron illustrates one-way MOOCs can be used as an equaliser to ease transition. Learning at a distance is helpful for people who are moving from one geographic location to another and the in-person learner support helps refugees not only to learn the academic subject but to orientate themselves in their new place of residence, supporting their development and helping them to become productive and participate equally within society.

In countries such as India, where the higher education system needs to be expanded rapidly, expansion of education largely is through private providers that tend to be confined to narrow professional tracks and are regulated through weak internal and state governance. In 2013, almost 90% of Indian colleges were rated as below average on quality parameters. MOOCs are viewed as a way to alleviate some of India's access and quality issues in higher education by enabling larger groups of people to have access to high quality learning. This expansion of education is particularly important for under-represented groups within Indian society. However, most MOOC participants in India are already well educated and live within the urban areas, reflecting learner trends from around the world. Expanding access requires MOOC providers to understand the needs of people in poorer, rural areas who have limited access to the internet and to technology devices that allow them to learn online. US-based MOOC provider edX has formed partnerships with Indian Institutions, including the Indian Institute of Technology in Bombay, to help them understand how they can provide MOOCs for under-represented groups in India. The British Council and the Open University is also working with Indian University Vice Chancellors to find solutions to expanding education in India. More examples like these of the use of MOOCs to equalise participation in society would help build the case for MOOCs as a democratising force worldwide, rather than as a form of control.

6.3   MOOCs as a Disrupting, not Reinforcing, Influence

MOOCs are configured to subvert the conventional social order of education (Siemens et al. 2010; Downes 2011). Yet, in some ways, they reinforce traditional patterns and behaviours in education. This effect is apparent from the earliest Connectivist MOOCs (cMOOCs) described in the previous chapters. The degree to which cMOOCs disrupt education, particularly their openness to different modes of behaviour, can be contested. They do not always allow for learner autonomy, as there is an expectation, by the MOOC facilitators and by some of the participants, that learners will adhere to prescribed 'norms' of behaviour. This issue is illustrated through a study of self-regulated learning in the Change11 MOOC (Milligan et al. 2013).

Change11 was a MOOC that took place over 35 weeks, from September 2011 to May 2012, with more than 2300 participants. The MOOC environment comprised an informal network with a variety of loosely connected digital platforms and tools including a registration portal, weekly online seminars and a range of blogs, tweets, videos and other materials from the instructors. A newsletter emailed daily to every registered participant included course announcements, links to blog posts and tweets from the participants. A link to any social media post from a participant using the hashtag#change11 was included in the newsletter.

There were three types of participation in the MOOC: active, passive and invisible. Active participants created and shared knowledge as blogs, tweets or comments on other's postings, created as original thought pieces or as spontaneous responses to other people's ideas. One active participant described his engagement, commenting, *"I have no idea how scattered I am across this MOOC, I have no idea how many contributions I've made, 30? 50? I've got a lot of replies ... I usually end a reply on an open end [to encourage a response]"* (P05).

A 'passive' participant explained her reservations about engaging in the MOOC: *"Sure, I can read other people's blogs and that's not a problem and I comment occasionally, but as far as really putting my ideas out there in the open in my own blog to be trampled on, you know there's a bit of fear there I think that I have and so that has been difficult for me"* (P12). This reticence led to her being less visible to other participants. From a learning analytics perspective, she may have seemed less engaged than other participants. However, in her view, she was learning.

Invisible learners included participants who chose to drop in and out of the MOOC, observing what was happening within the network but not contributing directly. One participant described this behaviour as *"hugely beneficial. Knowledge is filtered by the course organisers and has more value than something I randomly come across on the Internet"* (P18). Some who were inactive within the Change11 network were discussing the course with other people offline, or engaging in 'closed' social media groups, on Facebook or other platforms. They learnt within small, circumspect groups instead of openly contributing ideas to the network. Change11 participants who were openly and actively contributing ideas to the network were frustrated with these seemingly inactive members. Nevertheless, both groups—those who openly posted ideas and those who worked in smaller, closed groups—were learning in ways that suited their personal needs.

At one level, the contribution of knowledge by different people is based on a democratic assemblage, where educational hierarchy is replaced by a flatter, more horizontal structure. However, there are concerns that active participants are being deprived of the insights from the invisible participants. Do all participants have a duty to contribute to the dialogue in a MOOC in ways that allow others to learn from their experiences? Is there a responsibility for every MOOC learner to be, at the same time, a MOOC teacher. For MOOCs to become democratic spaces should learners have the freedom to participate in a MOOC in the ways that are meaningful to them, rather than in ways stipulated by the tutors?

Ideally, everyone in the MOOC would have the confidence and ability to be able to put forward and test their own ideas and understanding. For passive participants, an inability to contribute knowledge could be considered a form of illiteracy that diminishes the democratic power of a MOOC. By never contributing, these partici-pants are also not learning how to overcome that illiteracy. It could be argued that, to enable MOOCs as democratic spaces, effort should be put into ensuring everyone has the ability to contribute visibly. Equally, it could be contended that, in a democracy, everyone should be able to participate as they choose. And there is ample evidence to suggest passive participants are learning and gaining benefits.

Downes (2011) identified four important characteristics of cMOOCs—autonomy, diversity, openness and interactivity. However, autonomy and diversity in participation lead to tensions within the MOOC. Ideally in a cMOOC each learner is expected to contribute to the learning of other people through interactions and collective knowledge building activities. However, this expectation prevents some learners from autonomously learning outside the MOOC (Mackness et al. 2010). There is an expectation by the MOOC designers and some of the learners that participants will conform to the tacit 'norms' of the MOOC by behaving as visible and active participants. Thus, although notionally participant can learn autonomously in a MOOC, tensions may arise when learners use different forms of participation. In this way, MOOCs reinforce some of the norms of education.

The previous chapters delineated the considerable potential of MOOCs to disrupt education. However, MOOC innovations are being stifled in some ways by the culture and values that pervade education, such that MOOC innovations appear to be at the margins of formal education. However, these cultural values and norms are less apparent where MOOCs are used to support professional learning, or learning for work.

Professional learning is important in a world characterised by new forms labour (Billett 2004). Hardt and Negri (2009) describe this transformation as a shift from 'material labour', where manufactured products are created by a stable workforce, to 'immaterial labour', where the provision of new services and knowledge supersedes the production of material goods. Consequently, workplaces in many countries have moved from being structured around production models, to being characterised by flow of people, information and knowledge, which are fast, dynamic and disorderly. Information and knowledge is now available as digital resources, used as mediating artefacts or 'social objects' to connect people as they work (Engeström 2005; Knorr-Cetina 2001). It is the social interactions around MOOC resources that form a basis for new teaching models (Ferguson and Sharples 2014), rather than the availability of the MOOC itself.

Professional learning has been a growth area for MOOCs. Scenarios where MOOC learning is integrated within work practice, and where people learn through social, online interactions around their work activities, rather than in a standalone course, provide a learning model that is disrupting professional training. Coursera has been one of the first movers in this area, closely followed by edX and FutureLearn. There are also examples of courses for professionals (or people training to become a professional) that were offered independent of the mainstream MOOC platforms. These include the Midwifery MOOC described in the case example below.

Case Example: Integrating MOOC learning and work

The Evidence-Based Midwifery Practice MOOC aimed to support midwives, midwifery educators and other health professionals in clinical
practice to develop knowledge of evidence-based practice (http://www.
moocformidwives.com/). The course was designed and facilitated by professional midwives from the University of Aalborg in Denmark and the University
of Technology Sydney in Australia. The MOOC ran over a 6-week period in
April and May 2015 and attracted 2098 students from countries in Europe,
Asia, America, Africa and Australasia. It was comprised of six modules popu-
lated with a range of learning resources, including video lectures and scientific
articles (Dalsgaard and Littlejohn, in press). Regular, synchronous, online pre-
sentations were offered, and participants were expected to interact and share
knowledge on midwifery practice in their geographic location through online,
text-based forum discussions.

The MOOC created opportunities for professionals to integrate their work and
learning. Each participant had to explain customary midwifery practices in their
own country. They shared their viewpoints on distinctive forms of practice, and the
likely consequences in different regional settings. Sharing practice examples was a
good first step towards changing and improving practice. The MOOC is an example
of a community of networked expertise identified by Hakkarainen et al. (2004), where
professional learning is based around social interactions within a network.

In previous chapters, we described how access to resources alone is not sufficient
for learning and expertise development, since learning requires active agency of the
learner. Even the most promising structured online resources do not encapsulate the
knowledge needed to support learning and development. The case example illustrates how the midwives learned not only by accessing online learning resources, but
through social interactions and active exchange of knowledge.

The integrative pedagogies model for developing professional expertise identifies
four types of knowledge needed for learning: (1) conceptual and theoretical knowledge based on facts and concepts; (2) procedural or practical knowledge which
involves solving specialist, practical problems; and (3) sociocultural knowledge that
enables people to operate within a given cultural context; and (4) the self-regulative
knowledge needed to plan, perform and self-monitor development (Tynjälä et al.
2016). Formal education tends to focus on students learning conceptual and theoretical knowledge as well as procedural and practical knowledge. Over past decades,
formal education has been expended to include opportunities to learn sociocultural
and self-regulative knowledge. MOOCs can continue this trajectory when they serve
as a focal point for the coordination of activities that support the development of all
four types of knowledge. As learners gain expertise, there is a qualitative change in
the way they use the resources in a MOOC to learn, moving from rule-based actions
to fluid, self-directed activities (Dreyfus and Dreyfus 2005). To support learning
of thee different types of knowledge, MOOCs have to be designed as participatory

spaces, rather than as a set of 'learning materials' and products in the conventional sense. However, there has to be tolerance of learners who choose to participate in different ways, as illustrated in the previous section.

Professional learning has been a growth area for MOOCs. The focus has been on providing MOOCs for companies and public organisations. For example, the UK's tax office, Her Majesty's Revenue and Customs (HMRC), offer MOOCs to employees as a form of regular professional development. There are many growth areas where MOOCs can aid professional learning. For example, combining work and learning, as illustrated in the case example illustrating how midwives around the world could share practice examples. Another potential growth area is the 'gig-economy', companies such as Uber, Air B & B, and Mechanical Turk, where people are paid per task and need to learn on a just-in-time basis (Nickerson 2013). Gig economy workers could benefit, not only by using MOOC resources, but by participating in communities of networked expertise that could be associated with MOOCs. There is lots of scope for MOOCs to disrupt, rather than replicate, forms of online learning.

6.4 Opportunities for All: Supporting Self-regulation

MOOCs are positioned as a way for anyone, anywhere to access university education in ways that are 'equivalent to the on-campus experience'. The marketing documents from the MOOC providers claim MOOCs open up universities to students globally so they can become equal members of the academic community. This approach is particularly appealing for people who would like to study at an elite university, but have limited access to education. Nevertheless, there is a danger.

In Chap. 2, we described why learning online in a MOOC should not be viewed as being equivalent or comparable to on-campus learning. The view of a MOOC as being similar to a formal university 'course' places limitations on the benefits of MOOCs for students and for society. Learners could be liberated from having to follow a formal course pathway. And there are benefits for society when citizens can identify gaps in their knowledge and actively pursue ways to fill these gaps.

Learning in a MOOC is qualitatively different from learning face-to-face in a geographically based location and usually is not even equivalent to open, online learning at scale at an Open University. A critical aspect of learning on campus or at an open university is the support and feedback from tutors and peers, i.e. being a part of an academic community. Open University modules and degrees have high levels of support from tutors (academic support), and from student support teams (pastoral and other support), which have been termed 'supported open learning'. Most universities offer tutor-based support and, crucially, students learn within a community of scholars and peers. This form of support is missing or is truncated in a MOOC.

To participate effectively in a MOOC, learners have to engage actively (although not always collaborative). Chapter 4 provided ample evidence that not all learners are able (or want) to do this. Many do not have the cognitive, behavioural or affective characteristics necessary to be active agents determining their own learning pathways (Illeris 2007; Littlejohn et al. 2016). It seems MOOCs privilege those who are able to plan, perform and self-regulate their learning. There is a danger that the expansion of MOOCs inadvertently will lead to a form of discrimination, where those who are unable or unwilling to direct their own learning will not have access to the teaching support they require.

This disparity allows those who are able to self-regulate to overly influence what is happening and what is being learned in the MOOC (Milligan et al. 2013). It illustrates the 'inequalities of participation' Selwyn (2016, p. 31) warns of, where the experiences and outcomes of participating in learning will differ considerably depending on who the person is. If MOOCs are to be part of the shift towards 'learnification', where lifelong learners decide what, when and where they will learn, a critical element that has to be taken into consideration is the ability of learners to learn autonomously.

The ability to learn autonomously should be viewed as a critical literacy in a world where open, online, learning is becoming significant. In the past, governments have focused on critical literacies as a foundation of democracy and engagement in society and should similarly take action ensure all citizens are able to self-regulate their own learning in unstructured, online settings. There are a number of competency frameworks that guide education (see for example Voogt and Roblin 2012). Some frameworks emphasise self-regulation as a critical literacy. The expansion of MOOCs and other forms of open, online education means that self-regulation will increase in importance as a critical literacy. Otherwise, MOOCs and open, online education will serve to exacerbate, rather than alleviate, the equity issues in education.

One problem is that providing opportunities for learners to develop self-regulation ability can be complex and expensive. This is a particularly troublesome issue where MOOCs are seen as a cost-effective way to educate the masses. However, online learning should be valued for the unique ways it can support self-regulation through social interactions (Nicol and Macfarlaine-Dick 2006). MOOCs could liberate learning by encouraging learners to self-determine their learning pathway, while supporting self-regulation. Therefore, it is crucial to move away from the narrow focus on course provision and data-driven support towards preparing learners to be able to set and follow their own ambitions in unstructured open, online environments.

6.5 Rethinking Success Measures

The introduction of MOOCs has been associated with forms of economic growth. MOOCs may be viewed as a product that can be sold to student consumers. MOOCs can also be considered a new form of 'migration', allowing people to study for degrees in western universities, retaining the currency of a 'western degree' as superior to degrees from other countries, rather than supporting the improvement of universities around the world. Universities and businesses increasingly see MOOCs as part of a new currency at the heart of generating income streams, where students buy resources and qualifications. This may explain to some extent why MOOCs reinforce the idea of trading educational resources and formal, undergraduate education, rather than as a way to support societal learning in radically new ways. Tracing the evolving business model that supports the MOOC platform provider FutureLearn exemplifies these issues.

When the FutureLearn MOOC platform was introduced in 2012, it was based on a 'freemium' model. The aim was to increase interest in the partner universities by offering MOOCs as a taster and first step towards paid-for education. Although it is clear that a well-designed MOOC can reinforce the value of a university's 'brand', the monetary benefits from follow-through registration are difficult to calculate, and good return on investment is difficult to achieve. It is challenging to identify the number of students who register and pay for a course after experiencing a MOOC for free, since some of them may already have intended to study. The FutureLearn business model is evolving. Along with partner universities Deakin (Australia) and Coventry (UK), FutureLearn is currently experimenting with a new business model that allows students to try taster courses for free, then register for MOOC-style university degree programmes, as illustrated in the case example below:

Case Example: MOOCs as Deakin University Degrees

Deakin University in Australia is offering bachelor degrees on the Future-Learn platform. Students can begin their study by participating in short 'taster' courses that are free of charge, before enrolling in the Bachelors programme for a fee. The credits from the MOOC course go towards the degree. The programme is comprised of sequences, short MOOCs with assessments at the end of each course. FutureLearn describes this experience as 'the equivalent of a university subject'. Degrees are available in a range of subjects including Cyber Security, Information Technology, Financial Planning, Humanitarian and Development Action, Property and Diabetes Education. Deakin and FutureLearn are not the first to offer MOOC-based degrees. Coursera, edX and Udacity have all hosted Master's level offerings. These degree-based MOOCs have allowed universities and platform providers to experiment with revenue generation and expand MOOC business models to include new business lines.

The perspective of a MOOC as a retail commodity available on demand to customers does not take into consideration what is lost when learning solely is online, in particular the role of in-person, social interaction with tutors and peers. There are also ethical implications, especially transparency around what is being 'sold' to students. Organisations need to be clear that the online learning experiences are not equivalent to on-campus learning in terms of the qualitative experience.

It is not only the learners who need to understand what MOOCs do and do not offer, employers also need to be made aware of what the new 'currency' of MOOC qualifications and 'micro-credentialing' signal. These achievements could be merely a reinforcement and replication of traditional education; on the other hand, these new forms of credentialing could be implemented in ways that are more democratic and radically different from conventional education.

This view of MOOCs run the risk of narrowly focusing on success measures that are based around the learner's progress through a course—measures of progression, retention, assessment scores and time in a digital learning platform. These measures might not align with the learner's intentions, especially if he or she wants to learn a concept then leave the course. There is a danger that 'automated detectors of affect with nudges to promote growth mindset' may result in attempts to quantify learners' emotions and correct these to fit the 'ideal' psychological character. Numbers sometimes give an illusion of confidence, power and authority, whether their measures are representative of complex learning situations or not.

Broader signifiers of success are being explored in the literature, such as learner agency and the ability of learners to self-regulate their own learning. New analysis techniques are being developed to examine whether and how participants learn in online forums (Gillani and Eynon 2014), how they interact with intelligent tutoring systems (Wen et al. 2014), their self-regulation patterns (Siadaty et al. 2012) and their confidence and emotions (Dillon et al. 2016). The data from these analytics techniques allow the development of automated scaffolds and prompts. However, even these broad signifiers should be considered carefully because of complications in assessing whether a scaffold supports better learning, since not every student wants to reach the same endpoint. It is also difficult to pinpoint which factors actually are influencing learning processes. Therefore, we have to be careful about the assumptions that underpin Artificial Intelligence (AI) and data-driven systems. Currently, AI systems cannot assess learner progress at a level that is comparable with a human. Therefore, a combination of automatic measurement and analysis along with self-report and learner decision-making provides a possible way forward, though learners need to have the ability to make decisions about their own learning based on these multimodal data. Therefore, there are two future areas for the development of data-analytics for MOOCs. First, we have to understand when are the critical moments when scaffolding can help learners. But at the same time we must also make sure learners have the decision-making skills to be able to use and act on analytics scaffolds. It is the human–computer interface that will make the biggest difference in the effectiveness of MOOCs to support learners in achieving their goals.

6.6 Concluding Thoughts

This book has traced contradictions associated with the expansion of MOOCs. In reconceptualising education as open, online learning, it is necessary to question not only what new educational models are being implemented, but also why these models, tools and processes are being introduced; how they will contribute to improvements in practice; and how they will create enhanced opportunities and outcomes for all learners. To fully understand these questions, it is necessary to look beyond MOOCs themselves to explore the contexts that are shaping and informing their development and design.

The democratising vision of MOOCs relates to Hardt and Negri's (2005) concept of 'the multitude', where large numbers of people self-organise within a network to generate and share 'common knowledge' in ways that create conditions to reduce oppressive forms of power. While an alluring idea, the evidence suggests that MOOCs typically favour the educated elite, and that the democratising vision belies the 'inequalities of participation' (Selwyn 2016, p. 31), and substantial variation in the experiences and outcomes of individual learners. That is, MOOCs, and online education more generally, struggles with the same issues of equity that 'traditional' education does.

Even when learners have the ability to learn autonomously, course designers and researchers too often expect learners to conform to the course norms and specific behaviour (for example, completing a course or being 'visible'). The systems underpinning MOOCs continue to present a singular, top-down perspective of learning. Rather than emancipating the learner to follow a self-determined pathway, the reliance on analytics-based scaffolds often subjugate learners into compliance rather than supporting them to follow their own paths. However, despite the above pessimism, this book has identified examples of particular MOOCs that have served to breakthrough some of the inequities facing education, for instance, for migrant or refugee learners, or in brokering professional connections between midwives in Europe and in Africa. These successes perhaps indicate that when utilised in particular contexts, for particular purposes and with particular populations, MOOCs do have the potential to fulfil some of their original promise.

There, however, remains a risk that rather than offering a fresh, democratic approach to education, MOOCs reproduce the tacit forms of control that underpin education systems. At the same time, MOOCs also sustain the traditional hierarchy within which the novice learner is subjugated to expert 'teachers' who work in a variety of roles: subject matter experts, course designers, data analysts and those who create educational platforms and tools. There is a need to rethink ways MOOCs and other forms of open, online learning can extend education not only within the narrow boundaries of formal education, but beyond these frontiers, in areas of informal, professional, networked community-based learning. Again, there are nascent examples of these types of opportunities becoming available. Perhaps most promising are the informal, self-organising groups and participatory learning opportunities that would not be termed MOOCs but provide interesting case studies to understand how access can be opened and learning becomes a more reciprocal process distributed across users. In these instances, the open, distributed and collaborative possibilities offered by the Internet are leveraged without the influence of formal or traditional institutional structures.

Open, online learning has the potential to extend across every part of a learner's life. So, rather than focusing narrowly on how each learner fits within online education, we must consider how this reconceptualisation of learning fits within each learner's lifecycle. Rather than concentrating on offering materials, courses and services to the consumer student, we should take steps to ensure every learner has equal opportunities to learn from and contribute to new emerging forms of open, online learning. The ideas behind the 'personalization' movement in the compulsory sector apply to MOOCs and other forms of online education. More problematic perhaps, is that increasing evidence suggests that what makes personalization most successful in schooling contexts is the presence of strong relational support networks to support the student/learner through their learning journey.

These observations have a broader resonance with education in general, as MOOCs become synonymous with almost any type of online learning. It is clear that education systems, in their traditional forms, are not structured to facilitate the range of learning opportunities that are required in the twenty-first century. MOOCs, and open online learning in general, are providing exciting new models of learning. However, as this book has explored, while these models create new opportunities, in many cases they simply are reinforcing traditional educational models and outdated hierarchies in education. It is vital to reconceptualise learning in the digital age to harness the democratising potential of MOOCs.

Acknowledgements The authors wish to thank Vicky Murphy of The Open University for comments and for proofing this chapter.

References

Billett, S. (2004). Workplace participatory practices: Conceptualising workplaces as learning environments. *Journal of Workplace Learning, 16*(6), 312–324.

Dillon, J., Bosch, N., Chetlur, M., Wanigasekara, N., Ambrose, G. A., Sengupta, B., & D'Mello, S. K. (2016). Student emotion, co-occurrence, and dropout in a MOOC context. In *EDM* (pp. 353–357).

Downes, S. (2011). The MOOC guide. Retrieved from https://sites.google.com/site/themoocguide/home.

Dreyfus, H. L., & Dreyfus, S. E. (2005). Peripheral vision: Expertise in real world contexts. *Organization Studies, 26*(5), 779–792.

Engeström, Y. (2005). *Developmental work research: Expanding activity theory in practice* (Vol. 12). Berlin, Germany: Lehmanns Media.

Ferguson, R., & Sharples, M. (2014, September 16–19). Innovative pedagogy at massive scale: Teaching and learning in MOOCs. In C. Rensing, S. de Freitas, T. Ley, & P. J. Muñoz-Merino (Eds.), *Open learning and teaching in educational communities*. Paper presented at 9th European Conference on Technology Enhanced Learning, Graz, Austria (pp. 98–111). Cham, Germany: Springer.

Gillani, N., & Eynon, R. (2014). Communication patterns in massively open online courses. *The Internet and Higher Education, 23*, 18–26.

Hakkarainen, K. P., Palonen, T., Paavola, S., & Lehtinen, E. (2004). Communities of networked expertise: Professional and educational perspectives.

Hardt, M., & Negri, A. (2005). *Multitude: War and democracy in the age of empire*. New York, NY: Penguin.

Hardt, M., & Negri, A. (2009). *Commonwealth*. Boston, MA: Harvard University Press.

Illeris, K. (2007). *How we learn: Learning and non-learning in school and beyond*. London, UK: Routledge.

Knorr-Cetina, K. K. (2001). Postsocial relations: Theorizing sociality in a postsocial environment. In B. Smart & G. Ritzer (Eds.), *Handbook of social theory* (pp. 520–537). London, UK: Sage Publications.

Littlejohn, A., Hood, N., Milligan, C., & Mustain, P. (2016). Learning in MOOCs: Motivations and self-regulated learning in MOOCs. *The Internet and Higher Education, 29,* 40–48.

Mackness, J., Mak, S., & Williams, R. (2010, May 3–4). The ideals and reality of participating in a MOOC. In *Proceedings of the 7th International Conference on Networked Learning 2010,* (pp. 266–275). Lancaster: University of Lancaster.

Milligan, C., Littlejohn, A., & Margaryan, A. (2013). Patterns of engagement in connectivist MOOCs. *Journal of Online Learning and Teaching, 9*(2), 149.

Nickerson, J. (2013). Crowd Work and Collective Learning. In A. Littlejohn & A. Margaryan (Eds.), *Technology-enhanced Professional Learning* (pp. 39–50). Routledge: NY.

Nicol, D. J., & Macfarlane-Dick, D. (2006). Formative assessment and self-regulated learning: A model and seven principles of good feedback practice. *Studies in Higher Education, 31*(2), 199–218.

Selwyn, N. (2016). *Is technology good for education.* Cambridge, UK: Polity Books.

Siadaty, M., Gasevic, D., Jovanovic, J., Pata, K., Milikic, N., Holocher-Ertl, T., … & Hatala, M. (2012). Self-regulated workplace learning: A pedagogical framework and semantic web-based environment. *Journal of Educational Technology & Society, 15*(4), 75.

Siemens, G., Downes, S., Cormier, D., & Kop, R. (2010). PLENK 2010–Personal learning environments, networks and knowledge. Retrieved from http://connect.downes.ca/.

Tynjälä, P., Virtanen, A., Klemola, U., Kostiainen, E., & Rasku-Puttonen, H. (2016). Developing social competence and other generic skills in teacher education: Applying the model of integrative pedagogy. *European Journal of Teacher Education, 39*(3), 368–387.

Voogt, J., & Roblin, N. P. (2012). A comparative analysis of international frameworks for 21st century competences: Implications for national curriculum policies. *Journal of Curriculum Studies, 44*(3), 299–321.

Wen, M., Yang, D., & Rose, C. (2014, July). Sentiment analysis in MOOC discussion forums: What does it tell us? In *Educational Data Mining 2014.*